THE JEWISH PSEUDEPIGRAPHA

An introduction to the literature of the Second Temple period

SUSAN DOCHERTY

Fortress Press

Minneapolis

THE JEWISH PSEUDEPIGRAPHA
An Introduction to the Literature of the Second Temple Period

Fortress Press Edition © 2015

The publisher and author acknowledge with thanks permission to reproduce extracts from the following: The extract from Howard Jacobson, *The Exagoge of Ezekiel* (1982) is reproduced by permission of Cambridge University Press. J. H. Charlesworth (ed.), *The Old Testament Pseudepigrapha*, 2 vols (1983 and 1985): permission sought from Yale University Press. Every effort has been made to seek permission to use copyright material reproduced in this book. The publisher apologizes for those cases where permission might not have been sought and, if notified, will formally seek permission at the earliest opportunity.

Cover design: Joe Reinke
Cover image: Photograph taken by Mark A. Wilson (Department of Geology, The College of Wooster). Public domain.

Library of Congress Cataloging-in-Publication Data
Print ISBN: 978-1-4514-9028-2
eBook ISBN: 978-1-4514-9672-7

The paper used in this publication meets the minimum requirements of American National Standard for Information Sciences — Permanence of Paper for Printed Library Materials, ANSI Z329.48-1984.

Manufactured in the U.S.

For Ann and Laurence

Contents

Contents

Abbreviations

1QH	*Thanksgiving Hymns*
1QM	*War Scroll*
1QpHab	*Pesher Habakkuk*
1QS	*Community Rule*
11QT	*Temple Scroll*
Ant.	Josephus, *Jewish Antiquities*
Apoc. Ab.	*Apocalypse of Abraham*
b. Ber.	Berakot (Babylonian Talmud)
b. Sanh.	Sanhedrin (Babylonian Talmud)
b. Yoma	Yoma (Babylonian Talmud)
2 Bar.	*2 Baruch*
4 Bar.	*4 Baruch (Paraleipomena of Jeremiah)*
Barn.	*Epistle of Barnabas*
CD	Cairo Genizah copy of the *Damascus Document*
1 En.	*1 Enoch*
2 En.	*2 Enoch*
Fug.	Philo, *On Flight and Finding*
JJS	*Journal of Jewish Studies*
Jos. Asen.	*Joseph and Aseneth*
JSJ	*Journal for the Study of Judaism in the Persian, Hellenistic, and Roman Period*
JSP	*Journal for the Study of the Pseudepigrapha*
Jub.	*Book of Jubilees*
J.W.	Josephus, *The Jewish War*
L.A.B.	*Liber Antiquitatum Biblicarum* (Pseudo-Philo)
Let. Aris.	*Letter of Aristeas*
1 Macc.	1 Maccabees
2 Macc.	2 Maccabees
NTS	*New Testament Studies*
Pss. Sol.	*Psalms of Solomon*
QG	Philo, *Questions on Genesis*
SBL	Society of Biblical Literature

Sib. Or.	*Sibylline Oracles*
Sir.	Sirach/Ecclesiasticus
Spec.	Philo, *On the Special Laws*
T. Ab.	*Testament of Abraham*
T. Ash.	*Testament of Asher*
T. Benj.	*Testament of Benjamin*
T. Dan	*Testament of Dan*
T. Gad	*Testament of Gad*
T. Iss.	*Testament of Issachar*
T. Job	*Testament of Job*
T. Jos.	*Testament of Joseph*
T. Jud.	*Testament of Judah*
T. Levi	*Testament of Levi*
T. Mos.	*Testament of Moses*
T. Naph.	*Testament of Naphtali*
T. Reu.	*Testament of Reuben*
T. Sim.	*Testament of Simeon*
T. Zeb.	*Testament of Zebulon*
Wisd.	Wisdom of Solomon

1

Introduction

Introducing the Pseudepigrapha

The religion of Judaism is renowned for its literary output, and is particularly closely associated with the books of the Hebrew Bible and the later rabbinic literature. In addition, the media has brought to public attention in recent decades the important discovery of a large cache of ancient scrolls in caves at Qumran in the vicinity of the Dead Sea, while the works of the first-century authors Philo and Josephus have long served as important sources of information about Judaism in the New Testament era. A great wealth of other texts were composed by Jews in the centuries 'between the testaments', however, which are not so well known or widely appreciated today. It is these books, generally termed the Pseudepigrapha, which are the subject of this volume. They employ a wide range of genres to express theological ideas, promote certain values, explain the Scriptures, educate both Jews and gentiles about Jewish history and practices, and simply provide entertainment. Some of them, like *Jubilees* or *1 Enoch*, may have circulated widely and enjoyed an authority on a par with that of the writings which would eventually attain scriptural status. Some, such as the *Psalms of Solomon*, are liturgical texts, while others take the form of novels or plays, like *Joseph and Aseneth*, or the *Exagoge* by Ezekiel the Tragedian. All, however, are of immense value for an understanding of Second Temple Judaism and of the early Christian movement which arose within that religious and cultural context.

The term 'pseudepigraphic' is traditionally applied to these books because many of them are pseudonymous, which means that they are attributed to ancient and honoured figures from Israel's past, like Moses or Enoch. Others have no named author, and these features of pseudonymity and anonymity are very widespread in early Jewish literature, characterizing, for instance, the rabbinic literature, the Dead Sea Scrolls and the Apocrypha. These practices may be due to the imitation of scriptural models, in which authorship is not always

1

specified, or they may reflect the writers' belief that they were not putting forward their own views, but legitimately updating and passing on the traditions of their community. Pseudonymity thus helps to validate a work, providing a sense of authority and antiquity for its theological views or scriptural interpretation, and connecting its audience to Israel's history. For example, 'Ezra', the name of the priestly scribe who, according to Scripture, played a significant role in leading and teaching the exiles who returned from Babylon to Judaea in the fifth century BCE, is a very fitting name with which to associate a book (*4 Ezra*) dealing with an analogous situation, the aftermath of the destruction of the Second Temple in the first century CE. The designation 'Pseudepigrapha' is a very broad and not always an exact description of this literature, but these writings do form a recognizable collection which is distinct from the Apocrypha. The apocryphal books are considered scriptural in some Christian traditions and are more generally accessible and more familiar than the Pseudepigrapha, so they are not treated in this volume.[1]

The time span covered by this corpus of literature runs from the end of the Babylonian exile in 539 BCE to approximately 100 CE, soon after the destruction of Jerusalem by the Romans in 70 CE. The Second Temple was in existence for most of this period, standing as the focus of Jewish national identity and religion. It is often difficult to date the Pseudepigrapha precisely, especially if they contain no clear references to recognizable historical events, or draw on pre-existing sources. Some may have attained their current form only after the end of the first century CE, for example, yet possibly were in circulation previously in a more primitive form, or else appear to contain earlier material. The decision has been taken here to err on the side of including such works, like the *Sibylline Oracles*, on the basis that they can provide useful information about the theological views and scriptural interpretation of some Jews in the late Second Temple period, provided that they are approached with due caution, and the later date of their final form is acknowledged.

---

[1] The one exception is *4 Ezra*; this text is now incorporated into the Christian apocryphal work called 2 Esdras, but given that it is widely regarded as an important example of an early Jewish pseudepigraphic apocalypse and also that 2 Esdras is included in the Apocrypha but not the deutero-canonical Scriptures of the Roman Catholic Church, it seems appropriate to include it in this study (see Chapter 6).

It is also important to appreciate that these writings were preserved and transmitted mainly by Christian rather than Jewish communities, and that Christian revisions and additions have evidently been made to some of the original texts. This is, of course, part of a wider phenomenon, whereby Christianity absorbed and took over much of the Jewish literary and theological tradition, including the Scriptures, as it grew in both size and cultural and political influence. The question of the provenance of the Pseudepigrapha, then, is one with which contemporary scholarship continues to wrestle. In the past, all of these books were generally accepted as having been composed by Jewish authors, unless they contained obviously Christian material, such as references to Jesus, or to practices like baptism or the celebration of the Eucharist. Even then, these passages were widely regarded as Christian additions to an originally Jewish work. These assumptions are now, however, beginning to change. More recent commentators like James Davila and Robert Kraft have argued persuasively that the burden of proof should be shifted, and the Christian transmission of the Pseudepigrapha taken more seriously, so that all those writings which are not definitely Jewish in their theology should be considered as products of early Christianity, at least in their current form. It will be necessary to return to this debate at appropriate points in other chapters of this volume, but in general the approach taken here will be an inclusive one. Several of these disputed texts, such as the *Testaments of the Twelve Patriarchs*, will be discussed here, then, if they seem to contain older traditions reaching back to the Second Temple period or have close connections with other early Jewish writings, but the Christian influence on their final form will always be fully recognized.

There is a need to define one further term before proceeding. This Introduction has already referred several times to 'Scripture', but it is, strictly speaking, anachronistic to use this expression in relation to the Second Temple period, since all decisions about the form and constitution of the Jewish Scriptures were taken later. The authors of the rewritten Bible texts considered in Chapter 2 of this volume, therefore, were not rewriting Scripture as such, but interpreting texts which later came to be accepted as sacred by both Jews and Christians. It would be too cumbersome to repeatedly labour this point, so 'Scripture' will be used as a convenient shorthand throughout to refer to the writings which now comprise the Jewish Bible, but it should always be appreciated that the precise status and authority of the various religious writings in circulation at the time when the Pseudepigrapha were being composed was still undefined. A considerable fluidity and diversity of view persisted until the canon was fixed, but it is clear that the books of the Pentateuch gained a special place in Jewish thought at a relatively early date, and this is reflected in the fact that so much of the Second Temple Jewish literature draws on and interprets them.

The history of the Second Temple period

Jews in the land of Israel

The history of the people of Israel as it is recorded in the Scriptures is that of a tiny nation, often caught between the wars and ambitions of its larger neighbours. This pattern of Israelite subjection to powerful empires, such as the Babylonians, continued throughout the centuries, culminating in the invasion of Palestine by the advancing Roman armies in 63 BCE. The main extant sources of information for the Second Temple period are 1 and 2 Maccabees and the works of Josephus, although none of these writings can be taken as straightforward and historically accurate accounts. This era opens with Persia as the major regional force, and the exiles who wished to return to the small Persian-administered province of Judaea from Babylon being allowed to do so. Around two centuries later, the Persian Empire collapsed, having been defeated decisively by the forces of Alexander the Great in 331 BCE. This marked the start of the Hellenistic period, in which Greek language and education spread abroad throughout the known world. Some Jews apparently rejected Hellenism and all they thought it stood for, others probably embraced it enthusiastically, but for most it simply became the normative culture, inevitably adopted by all people in every region.

Judaea remained subject to Alexander's successors, the Ptolemies and Seleucids, for almost 200 years. The nation then achieved a brief measure of national independence when, prompted to some degree by the desecration of the Temple associated with the notorious Seleucid king Antiochus IV Epiphanes (175–164 BCE), an armed resistance movement led by the family of the Maccabees succeeded in overthrowing foreign rule and setting up a semi-autonomous state. From 141 to 63 BCE the priest-kings of the Maccabean or Hasmonaean dynasty ruled Judaea and eventually also its surrounding regions, including Galilee, Samaria and Idumaea. Even these years of greater independence were marred by battles abroad and strife at home, however, as the Jewish kings sought to expand their territory and deal with internal opposition and dynastic struggles. They were not universally popular with the inhabitants of Palestine, as they were not of the Davidic royal line, they assumed the role and title of high priest as well as king which was an innovation in Israelite practice, and they had to raise the money from taxation to fund their expensive wars. It is at this time that the existence is first attested of specific religious parties, the Pharisees, Sadducees and Essenes, who differed about various matters of theology and legal interpretation. The most famous area of disagreement, at least among readers of the New Testament, was the possibility of resurrection, but the members of these factions also held different views about such matters as fate and individual responsibility, the validity of the oral tradition, and the conduct of worship in the Jerusalem Temple.

Eventually, the Hasmonaeans were defeated by the Romans, who ruled Palestine first through client or puppet kings, and then through a series of provincial governors. Herod the Great (37–4 BCE) is the best known of the Roman-installed kings. He enjoys a reputation for great cruelty, and his reign certainly did provoke dissatisfaction among the populace, but he also completed several important rebuilding projects in and around Jerusalem and brought about some positive economic improvements in the region. The Roman officials who succeeded Herod's sons governed with varying degrees of efficiency, but they were distant from their subjects and often inept at dealing with Jewish unrest. Anger at the behaviour of these governors, socio-economic hardships and a desire for religious and national freedom all combined to incite a revolt against Roman rule in Judaea and Galilee in 66 CE. Armed resistance groups emerged to lead the fight against Roman forces, including the Zealots, whose name reflects the zeal with which they fought for their cause. The Jews were ultimately defeated by the Roman army, and Jerusalem was totally destroyed in 70 CE. Much of the city's population was forced into exile, and a new Roman colony was founded there, called Aelia

Capitolina. The Second Temple would never be rebuilt, and it would be 18 centuries before Jews began to return to Palestine in any numbers. This period of crisis is described at great length by Josephus in his book *The Jewish War*, and it forms the backdrop to several of the texts considered in this volume, especially the *Psalms of Solomon*, the *Testament of Moses*, *4 Ezra* and *2 Baruch*, which paint a distressing picture of a nation riven by war, factional strife, poverty and religious uncertainty.

Jews in the Diaspora

The great majority of Jews, however, did not live in Palestine but elsewhere in the Hellenistic world, at some remove from the events in Judaea. They are called the 'Diaspora' communities, a term derived from the Greek verb 'to scatter'. Many of the texts discussed in this volume reflect this context, and so provide significant evidence about Jewish life and thought in the Diaspora. A wide array of reasons, both political and economic, can be put forward to explain the extent of Jewish migration: movement from Palestine to Egypt in times of hardship appears to have been common even in biblical times, for example, and many of those exiled to Babylon in the sixth century BCE chose not to return. Other Jews in search of adventure and prosperity doubtless took advantage of opportunities on offer under various emperors to settle new colonies, or to gain employment as mercenaries. The numerous wars which were fought in these centuries, from Alexander the Great's ousting of the Persians, through the conflicts among his successors the Seleucids and Ptolemies, to the Roman invasions, led to the displacement of large numbers of people, including Jews, as prisoners or refugees. These and other factors contributed to the establishment of substantial Jewish communities in all the major cities of the Graeco-Roman Empire, including in Greece, Asia Minor, Italy, Syria and Egypt.

Many of these Diaspora Jews retained their traditional customs, practising circumcision, maintaining dietary regulations and celebrating Passover, for instance, and they continued to worship the God of their ancestors in their synagogues. That some of them retained an allegiance to the national homeland of Judaea is indicated by the annual collection of a tax from Jewish communities throughout the Mediterranean which was sent to Jerusalem for the upkeep of the

Temple. Pilgrimages to Jerusalem were also regularly undertaken, especially at festival times (e.g. Acts 2.5). However, the bulk of the evidence, from inscriptions and the extant writings of Jews and gentiles alike, suggests that generally they also felt part of the wider Hellenistic society in which they operated, and at home in its culture. Sources from Alexandria, where there was a particularly large Jewish population, indicate that Jews were accepted there as citizens, were able to play a full part in the life of the city, could own land and property and undertake a range of occupations, and that some benefitted from a classical education. Their inculturation is also indicated by the Septuagint translation of the Scriptures into Greek from the middle of the third century BCE, a process which presumably became necessary because they spoke no Hebrew. That Egyptian Jews at least regarded themselves as permanent residents in the Diaspora, not exiles with a constant yearning to return to Palestine, is also demonstrated by the building of a temple in Heliopolis in the late second century BCE, which stood for over two centuries, until it was closed by the Roman authorities in 73/74 CE.

Simple generalizations about Jewish life outside of Israel are best avoided, since the levels of tolerance and positive interaction with gentiles varied considerably in different regions and periods of time. Some Jewish practices certainly did provoke suspicion and prejudice among gentiles, particularly those which made normal social interaction difficult, such as dietary regulations and sabbath observance, and also circumcision, considered barbaric by many educated Greeks. In the case of disputes, however, extant records show the authorities usually upholding Jewish rights and accepting their distinctive religious customs. The presence of some ongoing tension between Jews and other citizens of the Graeco-Roman Empire is indicated by the fact that riots and persecution against Jewish communities broke out sporadically in different locations, including two incidents in Alexandria in the first century CE (37 CE and 66 CE). A significant number of Jews throughout Cyprus, Cyrene, Egypt and possibly Mesopotamia were also involved in an uprising against the authorities in 115/116 CE during the reign of the emperor Trajan. Nevertheless, sufficiently good relationships existed between Jews and gentiles in many Hellenistic cities for people to be attracted to Judaism. Such gentile 'godfearers' were evidently allowed to participate in worship and in the general life of the synagogue without fully converting or having to leave behind entirely their previous identity and associations. Some of the texts considered in this volume will be concerned with these questions of conversion and the relationships between Jews and gentiles, notably *Joseph and Aseneth* and the *Sibylline Oracles*.

Format and organization

There are various possible ways of organizing an introductory volume on the pseudepigraphic literature of the Second Temple period. One option is to treat the texts chronologically, in order of their composition date. This has the advantage of foregrounding their historical and social contexts, which often impact significantly on their theological emphases or literary forms. However, the problem with this approach is that so many of these writings cannot be dated precisely, or else were clearly composed in stages. It would become necessary, for example, to separate out into different chapters the individual books of the *Sibylline Oracles*, or the various sections of *1 Enoch*, which could prevent the reader from gaining an overall sense of the shape of these works and their contents.

A further possibility is to group the writings together according to the Old Testament character with whose name they are associated, or whom they particularly honour, such as Enoch, Abraham, Moses or Joseph. This can enable valuable comparisons to be drawn between different presentations of the same figure. However, this structuring method is also of limited use, because some characters, such as Job or Ezra, are linked with only one extant writing, while some texts, the *Sibylline Oracles*, for instance, have no connection with a particular person. In addition, it may lead the reader to miss important theological or literary aspects of a work by focusing unduly on the name attached to it. *Jubilees*, for example, styles itself as a divine revelation to Moses, but since it retells the whole of Genesis and the first part of Exodus, it is just as illuminating for its interpretation of Abraham and other patriarchs as of Moses.

The literature might also be divided along geographical lines, with different chapters covering, for example, texts composed in Palestine, in Egypt and elsewhere in the Diaspora. There are two serious issues with such an approach, however. In the first place, it is often impossible to locate these writings definitely in a particular city or country, since so little is known about their authors. Second, it can lead to the creation of an artificial division between 'Palestinian Judaism' and 'Diaspora Judaism'. The consensus of modern scholarship is that Jews in every part of the Graeco-Roman Empire, including the land of Israel, were influenced by Greek language, thought and culture, and therefore differences between the attitudes of Jews living in distinct regions should not be pressed too far. So, while texts written in Palestine may be characterized by some particular features, such as concerns about the conduct of Temple worship, or responses to Roman invasion, they are likely to share many theological ideas, ethical values and exegetical traditions in common with those deriving from the Diaspora.

This volume, therefore, is arranged around literary genres, so that each chapter deals with a different type of writing, such as rewritten Bible, testaments or apocalyptic. This format is not entirely without its difficulties, as many of the Pseudepigrapha exhibit features of more than one literary form, so their classification is not straightforward, and some genres are not very well established or easy to define, so that there is considerable debate about which works should be included in them. These points are acknowledged, where relevant, in the introduction to each section, and the understanding of 'genre' adopted here is necessarily broad. Despite the frequent use of mixed literary forms, this method of organizing the material remains the most practical and logical. Its particular advantages are that it is relatively easy for the reader to navigate; it highlights the creative use by the early Jewish writers of a variety of literary forms; it enables attention to be paid to all the noteworthy characteristics of each text; and it allows works which have something in common to be compared. Apocalyptic books do look and feel different from, for instance, biblical expansions, so a better appreciation of the nature and purpose of this type of writing can be achieved by considering the apocalypses together. Similarly, it is interesting to see how examples of the same form, such as rewritten Bible, differ from one another in their selection of material and emphases.

The main chapters in this volume will all follow a similar format, therefore, beginning with a brief overview of the literary genre under consideration, and moving to a more detailed discussion of the two, three or four main extant examples of it. An introduction to the authorship and historical context of each book will be provided, and then its key features, major theological themes, and interpretation of scriptural passages and themes will be explained. Since the Pseudepigrapha form part of a larger body of early Jewish writings, including the Apocrypha, the Dead Sea Scrolls, and the works of Josephus and Philo, every opportunity will be taken to identify connections, common themes and interesting differences between them and this wider literary corpus.

The significance of the Pseudepigrapha

A distinctive aspect of this introduction to the Pseudepigrapha is its focus on the significance of these texts, which will be highlighted at the end of every chapter. Their ongoing value is sometimes found in the theological and ethical teaching which they put forward, as many touch on issues which are as important now as they were two millennia ago, such as how to respond to social injustice, to the problem of innocent suffering or to the widespread human fear of death. This literature is also extremely important for what it reveals about the history, attitudes to Scripture, and rich and diverse theological tradition which characterized Judaism in the Second Temple era. This historical period is obviously of interest to classical scholars and students of Judaism, but is equally important for an understanding of early Christianity, which arose within the same social, cultural and religious milieu, and whose adherents preserved and valued these writings, a fact which is a telling reminder of the shared roots and close links between these two emerging religions. Their significance as evidence for the beliefs and practices of Christians in the early centuries of the Common Era, a time for which other sources of information are scarce, is, therefore, increasingly being recognized by scholars.

These texts are also relevant to several major current debates within the field of biblical studies, such as the relationship between Palestinian and Diaspora Judaism, and the formation of the Jewish Scriptures. Some of them are, of course, simply worth reading as good stories in their own right, able to entertain or move modern readers as they did ancient audiences. It is hoped, then, that this book will be able to offer a variety of persuasive answers to the important question of why anyone should still want to read the pseudepigraphic literature today.

Further reading

Charlesworth, J. H. (ed.), *The Old Testament Pseudepigrapha*. 2 vols. 1983 and 1985, New York: Doubleday

Collins, J. J. and Harlow, D. C. (eds), *Early Judaism: A Comprehensive Overview*. 2012, Grand Rapids, Michigan/Cambridge, UK: Eerdmans

Davila, J. R., *The Provenance of the Pseudepigrapha: Jewish, Christian or Other?* 2005, Leiden: Brill

Grabbe, L. L., *An Introduction to Second Temple Judaism*. 2010, London: T&T Clark

Gruen, E. S., *Diaspora: Jews amidst Greeks and Romans*. 2002, Cambridge: Harvard University Press

Samely, A. et al., *Typology of Anonymous and Pseudepigraphic Jewish Literature in Antiquity Project*. <www.alc.manchester.ac.uk/subjects/middleeasternstudies/research/projects/ancientjewishliterature>

Vanderkam, J. C., *An Introduction to Early Judaism*. 2001, Grand Rapids, Michigan/Cambridge, UK: Eerdmans

2

Rewritten Bible

Introducing the genre of rewritten Bible

Some early Jewish writings interpret the books which now make up the Bible by retelling parts of them, rather than commenting on them in the verse-plus-explanation format familiar from rabbinic sources and modern critical commentaries. Such rewriting of the Scriptures is, however, essentially the same kind of enterprise as formal commentary, as both seek to answer questions raised by the texts and to relate them to the issues of a new generation. It is also a very early form of exegesis, one which is found within the Bible itself: 1 and 2 Chronicles, for example, thoroughly rewrite and reinterpret the books of Samuel and Kings, traditions found in Exodus and Numbers are refashioned in Deuteronomy, and there are examples of the reuse and updating of older material throughout the prophetic books.[1]

The term 'rewritten Bible' as a description of this genre was coined in 1961 by the renowned scholar of early Judaism and Christianity, Geza Vermes, who defined it as 'a narrative that follows scripture but includes a substantial amount of supplements and interpretative developments'.[2] So, in these texts, sections of the biblical narrative are literally rewritten, mostly in the author's own words, but with some direct quotation and many echoes of scriptural language. The interpreter can, however, omit some episodes, drastically summarize others and include additions which offer a particular explanation of the underlying narrative. This extra material often serves to resolve apparent contradictions in the Bible, or to fill in gaps in the story, such as the names of minor figures or the inner motivation for a character's actions.

---

[1] Michael Fishbane has written extensively about this practice, called 'inner-biblical exegesis'; see e.g. his *Biblical Interpretation in Ancient Israel*. 1985, Oxford: Clarendon Press.

[2] G. Vermes, *Scripture and Tradition in Judaism*. 1961, Leiden: Brill, p. 95.

In the decades since Vermes' initial discussion of this genre, other scholars have defined its characteristics more fully. In an important study, for instance, Philip Alexander has concluded that rewritten Bible texts are always narratives, following a sequential, chronological order, and covering a substantial part of Scripture.[3] So, a work about one particular biblical figure which relates only minimally to the biblical narrative like *Joseph and Aseneth* would not be categorized as rewritten Bible by Alexander. The debate about the extent and the boundaries of this genre looks set to continue, focusing especially on whether it can also include rewritings of the legal sections of the Pentateuch, like the Qumran *Temple Scroll* (11QT).[4]

The best term to describe these texts is also a subject of debate, with the title 'rewritten Scripture' now generally preferred to 'rewritten Bible', since it avoids giving the misleading impression that a fixed 'Bible' with authoritative, canonical status had been agreed before these writings were composed. A further interesting question is why this form of biblical interpretation appears to have died out after the first century CE. One possibility is that with the establishment of the canon of Scripture and the stabilization of the biblical text at about this time, there was less scope for new presentations of its narrative. Certainly the structured verse-plus-comment format became the dominant form of interpretation in both rabbinic Judaism and early Christianity from this point on. In any case, the extant examples of this important genre illustrate the centrality for all Jews throughout the Second Temple period of the writings which would attain the status of Scripture: the underlying narrative of the Pentateuch in particular is presupposed in these rewritings of it; it is explicitly acknowledged in places (e.g. *L.A.B.* 43.4; 56.7; 63.5; *Jub.* 6.22); and there is a perceived need to root all theological ideas in its authority. Both the interpreters' exegetical creativity and their faithfulness to the traditions they have received, some of which seem to be very ancient, is apparent in these texts.

---

[3] P. S. Alexander, 'Retelling the Old Testament'. In *It Is Written: Scripture Citing Scripture: Essays in Honour of Barnabas Lindars*. Ed. D. A. Carson and H. G. M. Williamson. 1988, Cambridge: Cambridge University Press, pp. 99–118.

[4] See e.g. M. J. Bernstein, '"Rewritten Bible": A Generic Category Which Has Outlived Its Usefulness?' *Textus* 22 (2005), pp. 169–96.

The *Book of Jubilees*

Introduction to *Jubilees*

The *Book of Jubilees* retells the narrative of the book of Genesis and the early chapters of the book of Exodus, following the structure and wording of the biblical source very closely. It was composed in the middle of the second century BCE, somewhere between 160 and 130 BCE. This was a period of considerable political and religious turbulence in Palestine, when the Maccabees led a Jewish rebellion against the Seleucid ruler Antiochus IV Epiphanes. One of the leading scholars of *Jubilees*, James Vanderkam, has argued that the book may reflect a struggle between two groups of Jews which is hinted at in other writings dating from this time (e.g. 1 Macc. 1.11). It seems that there were some Jews who advocated a more accepting attitude towards Hellenization and desired to create better relations between Israel and other nations, even if this involved a relaxation of some of the more distinctive Jewish laws. On the other hand, there were those like the author of *Jubilees* who strongly opposed any such accommodation and stressed instead God's special covenant with Israel and the need to maintain a clear separation from gentile practices.[5] These differences of view led ultimately to the formation of parties within Judaism, such as the Essenes and the Pharisees.

Originally written in Hebrew, the book was translated into Greek, from Greek into Latin and also into the ancient Ethiopic language Ge'ez. The original Hebrew text was lost, but some quotations from *Jubilees* in Greek and Latin are found in the writings of the church fathers, evidence of its continuing popularity and influence. Fortunately the Ge'ez version survived in a more or less complete form, because it was transmitted throughout the centuries as part of the canon of Scripture in the Ethiopian Church. The discoveries at Qumran have since thrown further light on *Jubilees*, as 15 fragmentary copies of the book in Hebrew were found there. These manuscripts are important new evidence, showing first that the Ethiopic version was a generally faithful translation of the original Hebrew, and second that it was held in high regard by the Qumran

---

[5] J. C. Vanderkam, *The Book of Jubilees*. 2001, Sheffield: Sheffield Academic Press, pp. 139–41.

community. Indeed, there are notable parallels between *Jubilees* and some of the Dead Sea Scrolls, in the interpretation of various laws, for example, and in the adherence to a 364-day solar calendar rather than a lunar system for dating festivals.

Nothing definite is known about the author of *Jubilees*, but he is usually assumed to have lived in Palestine. He may also have come from a priestly family, given the priority he attaches to Levi (30.18; see also 45.15) and the attention he pays to ritual matters such as the celebration of festivals and the laws about sacrifices. Other Jewish writings of this period share similar traditions, enhancing Levi's role and significance, such as the *Aramaic Levi Document*, which may have been a source for *Jubilees*, or have emerged from the same kind of priestly circles.

The *Book of Jubilees* takes the form of an extended revelation to Moses by an angel, and includes a detailed account of Israel's history, of the covenant between God and Israel, and of important laws and their interpretation. It also foretells that the people will fail to keep all the demands of the covenant so will be punished and exiled, but will eventually be shown mercy by God and restored to their own land (see e.g. 1.7–18). This setting for the narrative gives it a great deal of authority, claiming for it a status equal to that of Scripture, since it is God who commands that its message be communicated to the great teacher Moses through a high-ranking angel (1.26–7). Its words therefore demand attentive obedience, especially as they were first inscribed on heavenly tablets (1.29). Most commentators agree, however, that the author did not regard his work as a replacement for the Scriptures, but rather as a supplement to or explanation of them, since he specifically refers his audience to what is written in the book of the first law (6.22; cf. 2.24; 30.12), presumably the Torah. It is possible that he understood his additional material to have formed part of God's revelation to Moses during the 40 days and nights he was said to have spent in God's presence on Mount Sinai (Exod. 24.18).

Key features of *Jubilees*

The underlying biblical narratives can be treated in a variety of ways in works of rewritten Bible. There is always a mixture of straightforward retelling, rewriting with minor or more substantial changes, summarizing, interpretative additions and omissions. So, almost all of the contents of Genesis 1 to Exodus 12 are reproduced in *Jubilees*, in the same sequential order, but some episodes are abbreviated (e.g. the Joseph stories, see especially 39.1–4; the account of the sending of the plagues on Egypt, 48.5–8), while others are expanded with extrabiblical traditions and the author's own interpretation (e.g. the creation account, chapters 2—3; Noah and the flood, 5.20—7.6; Abraham's youth, especially his early abhorrence of idolatry, 11.14—12.21).

The rewritten Bible genre also allows for the smoothing out of any inconsistencies or perceived difficulties in the original narrative. This feature is noticeable in *Jubilees*, in that, for instance, it is not said that Abraham pretended that his wife was his sister to secure his safety in Egypt (Gen. 12.10–20; cf. 20.2–7) but simply that Sarah was taken from him (13.13). In similar fashion, the text emphasizes Judah's repentance for having sexual relations with Tamar (41.23–4), and justifies Rebecca's favouritism for Jacob, on the basis of Esau's fierceness from birth (19.14) and ongoing disloyalty to his parents (25.1; cf. 29.16–20; 35.13–14). Connections can also be made between different passages of Scripture. In *Jubilees*, for example, a parallel is drawn between the drowning of the pursuing Egyptians at the time of the exodus and their killing all the baby Hebrew boys by throwing them into the river (48.14; cf. *L.A.B.* 9.10; Wisd. 18.5). This tendency to link apparently unrelated texts is even more pronounced in the *Biblical Antiquities* of Pseudo-Philo, discussed below, and is found in many forms of early Jewish interpretation, testifying to the way in which these exegetes were steeped in the knowledge of Scripture, and read it as an interconnected and coherent whole, paying attention to its every word.

Biblical interpretation often aims to bring a scriptural text up to date and relate it to the issues facing a contemporary audience. This goal, called actualization, is clearly in evidence in *Jubilees*, providing some clues to its historical setting. The account of Jacob's wars against the Amorites and Edomites (chapters 34 and 37—38), for example, may have been influenced by some of the battles in the recent past under the Maccabees, as a similar list of the allies of Israel's enemies is given in the report of the war between Judas Maccabeus and the

Idumaeans or Edomites in 1 Maccabees 5. The Edomites, regarded as the descendants of Esau, are presented in a more negative light in *Jubilees* than in Genesis, and these chapters seem to be an attempt to justify the hostile relations between Israel and Edom/Idumaea in the later period. *Jubilees* shows some interest in the emotions of scriptural characters, although this feature is not as pronounced as in the later writings of Josephus, who reflects the influence of contemporary Graeco-Roman literature in this regard. The author considers, for instance, how Abraham would have felt when he parted from Lot, given that he had no sons of his own (13.18). A further literary characteristic of rewritten Bible is the creation of speeches, through which the interpreter can explain the meaning of the narrative or give voice to some of his key theological ideas. Such insertions are found throughout *Jubilees*, often taking the form of prayers (e.g. by Noah at 10.3 and Abraham at 12.19–21), blessings (e.g. Terah on Abraham, 12.29; Abraham on Jacob, 19.26–9 and 22.11–23; Rebecca on Jacob, 25.15–23) or 'testaments' spoken by a patriarch as he is about to die (e.g. Noah, 7.20–39; Abraham, 20.1–10; 21.1–26; Isaac, 36.1–16). The author uses these speeches to stress the importance of faithfulness to the covenant and the Jewish law, and to urge the avoidance of idolatry and intermarriage with gentiles.

In these sections there is overlap with the testament genre (see below, Chapter 5), and rewritten Bible texts also have features in common with apocalyptic works (see below, Chapter 6). *Jubilees* is, for instance, pseudonymous, presents itself as a revelation mediated by an angel and, like many apocalypses, regards history as being divided up into distinct periods. It is not, however, characterized by extensive eschatological speculation, containing only one prediction of future apostasy, disasters and judgement (23.11–31). The apocalyptic writing with which *Jubilees* appears to have the closest relationship is *1 Enoch*. Thus the scanty biblical information about Enoch is enhanced in *Jubilees* with the details that he was the first person to learn to write, that he understood calendrical and astronomical matters, that he had knowledge revealed to him by angels and that he is even now recording the deeds of people for judgement (4.16–25; for further parallels with *1 Enoch* see e.g. 5.1–2; 7.20–9). There may be some literary dependence between the two texts, which probably works both ways, as *1 Enoch* is made up of five sections dating from different periods, some composed earlier than *Jubilees* and others later (see further below, Chapter 6).

Perhaps the most noticeable distinctive feature of *Jubilees* is the way in which the author links laws to scriptural texts and presents Israel's ancestors as keeping these statutes even before the time of the Sinai covenant. So, for example, the regulations about the purification of women after childbirth (see Lev. 12.2–5) are related to the creation narrative and the example of Adam and Eve in the Garden of Eden (3.8–14), and the actions of Dinah's brothers in avenging her rape by Shechem are used as justification for an eternal prohibition on Jews marrying gentiles (30.7–17; cf. Gen. 34.1–31). This technique serves to imbue the whole of Jewish law with full patriarchal authority.

It is also striking that the wives of all the key scriptural figures are named in *Jubilees*, and details provided of their paternal lineage. It seems that the author wishes to stress the genealogical purity of the line of Israelites through whom God established the covenant, which included no gentiles or others who might be considered unworthy (see e.g. 34.20–1 for a list of the names of the wives of the sons of Jacob). This feature has attracted the attention of scholars like Betsy Halpern-Amaru, who has examined in particular the reworking of the narratives about Isaac's wife Rebecca. She concludes that one of the messages of *Jubilees* is that marrying outside the nation – or even outside the extended family – will always result in negative consequences and is a threat to the ethnic purity of Israel. This, together with the book's emphasis on the importance of circumcision, leads her to suggest that it was written partly in response to a rise in gentile conversion in this period, and that its author belonged to a group which opposed this on principle and did not regard children born of Jewish men and gentile women as true Jews.[6] All the rewritten Bible texts show a similar concern to identify characters unnamed in the Bible and provide lists of the wives and children of Israel's ancestors, although they rarely agree on these names. Pseudo-Philo demonstrates an even greater interest in minor women characters than *Jubilees*, as will be seen in the discussion below of the *Biblical Antiquities*.

---

[6] B. Halpern-Amaru, *The Empowerment of Women in the Book of Jubilees*. 1999, Leiden: Brill; see esp. pp. 147–59.

Important themes in *Jubilees*

At the heart of the *Book of Jubilees* lies the theme of God's covenant relationship with the people of Israel. This special bond is traced right back to the time of creation, when God is depicted as saying to the angels: 'I shall separate for myself a people from among all the nations. And they will be my people and I will be their God' (2.19).[7] This covenant is first made with Noah (6.4), renewed with the patriarchs Abraham (14.20; 15.4) and Jacob (27.22–4), and God will be eternally faithful to it, despite the Israelites' many sins (e.g. 1.5). *Jubilees* is concerned to stress from the outset that God knew that the covenant people would go on to commit evil deeds (1.5–18), perhaps in response to developing theological questions about whether God was not powerful enough to control the chosen people, or had made a poor choice in the first place. Israel's divine right to inhabit the promised land is also defended, which may suggest that the author was responding to contemporary challenges to their ownership of it. The account of the division of the earth among Noah's descendants, for example, claims that the territory now occupied by the Jews had always been intended by God for the Israelites, but was wrongfully seized by Canaan for him and his descendants to dwell in, although he had other land assigned to him (10.27–34), so any Canaanite claim to it must be illegitimate.

This emphasis on covenant brings with it a focus on the laws which serve to maintain it. Thus the author exhorts his audience particularly forcefully to avoid idolatry (e.g. 1.8–11; 12.1–5; 36.5), intermarriage with gentiles (e.g. 20.4; 22.20; 25.1; 30.7–13) and any-thing which detracts from the distinctiveness and ethnic purity of Israel: 'Separate yourself from the gentiles . . . and do not perform deeds like theirs . . . because . . . all of their ways are contaminated, and despicable, and abominable' (22.16). This is one of the reasons why commentators suggest that *Jubilees* emerged from within circles of Jews who opposed any accommodation with the Hellenization programme of Antiochus IV Epiphanes and other foreign rulers. The text's warning against nakedness (3.31) may, for instance, be a response to the Graeco-Roman practice of exercising naked in the

---

[7] All translations of the text are taken from O.S. Wintermute, 'Jubilees'. In *The Old Testament Pseudepigrapha Vol. 2.* Ed J.H. Charlesworth. 1985, New York, Doubleday, pp. 35-142.

gymnasium, an institution apparently introduced into Jerusalem not long before *Jubilees* was written (see 1 Macc. 1.13–14; 2 Macc. 4.9–14).

Perhaps the most important laws for the author of *Jubilees* concern sabbath observance. The importance of this commandment is enhanced in a lengthy addition to the creation account (2.17–33), and the book closes with a detailed reminder of the sabbath laws and their solemnity (50.1–13). It is said that the angels kept the sabbath with God from the very beginning of creation (2.18, 30), and among humans its observance is presented as a special privilege of the Israelites: 'The creator of all blessed it [i.e. the seventh day], but he did not sanctify any people or nations to keep the sabbath thereon with the sole exception of Israel' (2.31; cf. 50.10). This emphasis may be a sign that these regulations were being contested at this time or that many Jews felt no need to keep them strictly. It may also indicate that the author was of priestly descent, as he shows particular interest in other ritual matters, too, such as circumcision (15.25–34) and the proper celebration of festivals like Passover (49.1–23). Levi, the first priest (30.18), is accorded particular prominence in *Jubilees*. When Jacob takes his sons to see his father Isaac, for instance, Levi is the first to receive his grandfather's blessing (31.11–17). In a significant statement about the role of the priestly line in transmitting Israel's ancient traditions, it is also claimed that before his death Jacob passed on to Levi books containing the patriarchal wisdom so that he might preserve them and renew them for his sons until this day' (45.15). Other ancestral figures like Adam and Enoch are seen acting like priests, offering incense and sacrifices, for example (3.27; 4.25).

One of the most striking characteristics of *Jubilees* is the repeated claim that the patriarchs celebrated the main festivals, like Firstfruits and the Day of Atonement, even though these feast days actually emerged at a later point in history (see e.g. 6.17–19; 15.1; 16.20–7; 22.1). This technique parallels the reading back into the patriarchal period of the laws first given at Sinai, discussed above, and it serves to highlight the antiquity and importance of these festivals, which may have been questioned by some Jews at the time. Significantly, it enables the author to give divine, scriptural authority to his interpretation of precisely how and when these days are to be celebrated.

This question of the correct calendrical system, and the related matter of chronology and dating, is another central theme in *Jubilees*. The book argues strongly for a 364-day solar calendar rather than one governed by the moon. In the account of creation, for example, it is explicitly stated that God gave the sun and not the moon the determining role in matters of festivals and dates (2.9; cf. 1.14). The rewritten Bible format enables the author to interweave his own views on this subject with the underlying biblical narrative; so, for instance, he inserts a lengthy warning about the dangers of failing to follow the solar calendar into a speech of God to Noah after the flood (6.32–8). A 364-day calendar is divisible into exactly 52 weeks, so all the festivals and other important dates fall on the same day of the week every year. In the view of the circles behind *Jubilees*, it was extremely important to know when to celebrate festivals, as their validity or the effectiveness of their rituals cannot be guaranteed unless they are celebrated on the correct, sacred day.

This solar calendar features in some of the Dead Sea Scrolls (e.g. *Psalms Scroll* 27.4–7; *Commentary on Genesis A* 2.2–3; cf. *Community Rule* 1.13–15; *Damascus Document* 6.18–19) and the Enochic literature (see especially *1 En.* 72—82), and is possibly presupposed also by parts of the Hebrew Bible, such as Chronicles, Ezra and Nehemiah, and Ezekiel.[8] It is, therefore, a very ancient system within Judaism, and it is likely that a wholesale move to a lunar calendar only came about at the time of Antiochus IV Epiphanes. The debate prompted by this change is reflected in texts such as Daniel 7.25, and it was apparently strenuously opposed by traditionalists such as those who stand behind the *Book of Jubilees*.

The solar calendar forms the basis for a wider chronological scheme, which is one of the most noteworthy aspects of the book. So each period of seven years is termed a 'week' of years, and each period of seven times a week of years, or 49 years, is called a 'jubilee'. More precise dates than those found in Scripture are given throughout *Jubilees*; so, for example, it was 'in the first year of the exodus of the children of Israel from Egypt, in the third month on the

---

[8] The theory that a solar calendar was used in Old Testament times has been defended in particular by Annie Jaubert, who has also argued that Jesus and his disciples followed this calendrical system; see her *La date de la cène: Calendrier biblique et liturgie chrétienne.* 1957, Paris: Gabalda.

sixteenth day of that month' (1.1) that God called Moses up to receive the law on Mount Sinai. In another example of this tendency, it is stated that Adam and Eve lived for exactly seven years in the Garden of Eden and left it after succumbing to the serpent's tempting on the first day of the fourth month (3.32; for further examples see 42.1; 45.11; 46.8; 47.1).

The activity of angels and evil spirits is taken for granted in *Jubilees*, as in the majority of other writings from the Second Temple period, but there is little interest in naming them or in distinguishing between their roles, so speculation in this area was perhaps at an early stage. Only Beliar (1.20) and Mastema the prince of evil spirits (e.g. 10.8; 11.5, 11; 48.2–19) are named; Mastema's role is particularly significant, as he is behind a plot to test Abraham by asking him to sacrifice Isaac (17.16; 18.12), and he tried to prevent Moses from freeing the Hebrew slaves at the time of the exodus (48.2–19). These spirits explain the presence of evil in a world created by a good God, because they are charged with leading people astray (e.g. 10.1–2; 11.4–5; 12.20), although the majority of them are now said to have been bound in the depths of the earth until the day of judgement (5.6–11; 10.7–9; cf. *1 En.* 10.12–13; 14.5).

The angels are introduced by their rank rather than by name, with the angels of the presence and the angels of sanctification being the most senior (e.g. 2.2, 18). Lesser angelic powers control the forces of nature within the world, such as wind, fire and the seasons (2.2), and teach skills to people (3.15). The creation account in *Jubilees* makes clear that the angels or spirits were actually created by God (2.2), so are not equal to God, and they have a particular role in ministering to God in heaven as priests do on earth (30.18). Israel is presented as the nation most similar to the angels, who are, for example, born circumcised (15.27), and who observe the sabbath in heaven (2.18).

Finally, the central role accorded to Jacob in *Jubilees* is noteworthy. Abraham interacts with Jacob in a way that he does not in the book of Genesis, where the report of Abraham's death (Gen. 25.7–10) precedes the announcement of the birth of Esau and Jacob (Gen. 25.19–27). In *Jubilees*, Abraham meets Jacob several times, blesses him more than once (e.g. 19.26–9; 22.10–30), and encourages his mother Rebecca to favour her younger son over his brother, as he knows that Jacob is the one through whom the covenant promises will be fulfilled (e.g. 19.17–25). The effect of this rewriting of the scriptural narrative is that Abraham is active for longer and Jacob becomes important sooner, which serves to minimize the role of Isaac. The reason for this emphasis on Jacob cannot now be identified with certainty, but it seems to relate to the author's view that the covenant is passed on through a pure line focused on key individuals like Abraham and Jacob, who were chosen and blessed by God.

The *Biblical Antiquities* of Pseudo-Philo

Introduction to the *Biblical Antiquities*

The *Biblical Antiquities* retells parts of the biblical narrative from the time of Adam to the rise of David and the death of Saul, employing a mixture of omission, summary and expansion of the scriptural material; very few episodes are retold without amendment. This work is rather longer than *Jubilees*, and the author focuses on some scriptural characters in particular, such as Moses and several of Israel's judges. Its author, known as Pseudo-Philo, does not begin with the account of creation, a narrative which is considerably developed in *Jubilees*, but he continues his account to a much later period of Israel's history. There is, then, a significant difference in the sections of Scripture chosen for retelling in the works of rewritten Bible, which can provide clues to their context and purpose.

For many centuries the *Biblical Antiquities* was ascribed to the well-known first-century Jewish writer Philo because its Latin version was preserved and transmitted together with Latin translations of Philo's works. It is therefore often still referred to by its Latin title, *Liber Antiquitatum Biblicarum*, or by the abbreviation *L.A.B.* This was a historical accident, however, as it was clearly not composed by Philo, who wrote in Greek and in a very different style. Instead, the author was probably a Jew who lived in Palestine and wrote in Hebrew; the work was then translated into Greek and from Greek into Latin.

There is a widespread scholarly consensus that the *Biblical Antiquities* is to be dated to the late first century CE, although there is less agreement about whether it comes from the years before or after the destruction of the Temple by the Romans in 70 CE. Verses such as 22.8, which speak of sacrifices being offered currently (cf. 26.15), imply that the Temple was still standing in the author's own time, and if the catastrophe of the fall of Jerusalem had occurred, it might be expected to loom more largely in the book, as it does, for example, in other works composed around 100 CE like *4 Ezra* or *2 Baruch*. On the other hand, Pseudo-Philo's emphasis on disasters as God's just punishment for sin, to be followed by mercy and restoration for Israel, is a message which would fit well with the situation post-70, when God's faithfulness to the covenant was called into question. In any case, the way in which this author interprets the Scriptures is of great interest to students of the New Testament, given its similar time of composition.

Key features of the *Biblical Antiquities*

The *Biblical Antiquities* illustrates admirably the mixture of expansion and abbreviation which characterizes the rewritten Bible genre. Many sections of the underlying scriptural source are heavily summarized, such as the Abraham cycle (8.1–3); the Joseph story (8.9–10); the account of the plagues which afflicted the Egyptians (10.1); and God's instructions for the building and furnishing of the Temple (11.15). It is no longer possible to be sure whether the author simply decided to condense material which he felt was generally very well known or unnecessarily repetitive, or if he had deeper reasons for playing down some parts of the biblical narrative. He clearly made a choice, however, to devote far more time and space to detailing the lives of Israel's judges and early kings – Samuel, Saul and David – figures whom he perhaps saw as having greater relevance for his audience. This aspect of the book suggests to some commentators that the question of Israel's leadership may have been a particularly pressing one for Pseudo-Philo. George Nickelsburg is particularly associated with the view that the author believed that the Jews of his day needed some bold, decisive, law-observant leaders like the ancient judges in order to deal with the threats they faced, whether from external aggressors or assimilationist tendencies within Israel.[9]

Significant characters like Abraham and Moses are treated in the *Biblical Antiquities*, as would be expected, but one of the most striking features of the work is the attention paid to other much more minor figures. Four whole chapters (25—28) are devoted to Kenaz, for instance, who is said to have assumed the leadership of Israel after the death of Joshua and single-handedly slain 45,000 Amorites. By contrast, the biblical account refers to Kenaz only in passing as the father of one of Israel's early judges, Othniel, and his brother Caleb (Judg. 3.9, 11). Moses' father, Amram, also plays a greater role in the narrative of Pseudo-Philo (9.3–9) than he does in the book of Exodus, where he receives only fleeting mention without being named (Exod. 2.1).

An interesting facet of this tendency to focus on minor characters is the prominence given to women in the *Biblical Antiquities*. A particularly clear example of this is the reworking of the story of Jephthah's daughter (Judg. 11; *L.A.B.* 40). The book of Judges describes Jephthah's battle against the Ammonites, and his vow to offer in sacrifice the first living creature from his household to meet him on his return from war if God should grant him victory over these enemies of Israel (Judg. 11.31). Tragically, it was his only child who came out first to greet him in a dance of welcome (Judg. 11.34). Pseudo-Philo retells this story in detail, placing much more emphasis on Jephthah's daughter, unnamed in Scripture, but here called Seila and given a far stronger identity. She makes a lengthy, poetic speech, expressing her sorrow about her father's vow (40.5–7), but also draws a parallel between herself and Isaac, who was likewise prepared as a sacrifice by his father, and she states her willing acceptance of her fate since it has brought about the freedom of her people (40.2–3). God's interesting response to Seila's words is to affirm: 'I have seen that the virgin is wise in contrast to her father and perceptive in contrast to all the wise men who are here . . . and her death will be precious before me always' (40.4).[10]

Deborah is also an important character in the *Biblical Antiquities*; four chapters are devoted to her (30—33), theologically significant

---

[9] See e.g. G. W. E. Nickelsburg and J. J. Collins (eds), *Ideal Figures in Ancient Judaism*. 1980, Ann Arbor, Michigan: Scholars Press.

[10] All translations of the text are taken from D.J. Harrington, 'Pseudo-Philo'. In *The Old Testament Pseudepigrapha Vol. 2*. Ed. J.H. Charlesworth. 1985, New York, Doubleday, pp. 297-377.

speeches are ascribed to her (e.g. 30.3–7), and she is said to 'enlighten' her people (30.2; cf. 33.1), a verb more usually associated with Moses (11.2; 12.2) or the law (11.1; 19.6; 23.10). Some intriguing plays on familiar biblical phrases appear throughout the book, such as the designation 'woman of God' for Deborah (33.1), and 'returning to the bosom of her mothers' as a euphemism for the death of Seila (40.4). These features have provoked discussion about the text's perspective on women, and the possibility of female authorship has even been floated. This seems highly unlikely in the culture of first-century Palestine, especially as an interest in female characters is not confined to the *Biblical Antiquities* and so appears to be part of a wider literary phenomenon: other examples of this within Jewish literature of the early post-biblical period include *Joseph and Aseneth*, the book of Judith and the story of Susanna.

Perhaps the most noteworthy feature of Pseudo-Philo's writing is the way he takes every opportunity to make connections between different parts of the Bible, both in terms of small details and also larger narratives and themes. This technique serves to creatively highlight the overall coherence of the Scriptures. An example of this form of biblical interpretation is the link he makes between the role of 'rods' in choosing the priestly tribe (Num. 17.6–10) and Jacob's use of 'rods' to produce more speckled animals from Laban's flocks (Gen. 30.37–39; *L.A.B.* 17.4). It is easy to see how this attentive reading of the text developed into the method of *gezera shawa* which occurs frequently in later rabbinic commentaries, in which one passage can be used to explain another if a similar word or phrase occurs in both. The frequent employment of this technique often results in episodes being told in the *Biblical Antiquities* in a different order from the scriptural narrative. The sealing of the covenant between God and Abraham (Gen. 15.1–21) is retold as part of the account of the later covenant renewal ceremony under Joshua (Josh. 24; *L.A.B.* 23.6), for instance, and the story of the near sacrifice of Isaac (Gen. 22.1–19) is included, with some elaboration, not as part of an account of Abraham's life, but in a later hymn uttered by Deborah (32.1–4).

Connections are often drawn also between biblical figures, as in the case of the parallel between Isaac and Jephthah's daughter (40.2) noted above. Similar links are made between Korah, who led a rebellion against Moses in the wilderness (Num. 16.1–50), and Cain, who murdered Abel (Gen. 4.1–16; *L.A.B.* 16.2), and between Saul and Jeremiah, who were both very young when they took on the roles of king and prophet respectively (56.6; cf. Jer. 1.6). Sometimes these connections take the form of contrasts rather than parallels, so that, for example, Samson is criticized for taking the Philistine Delilah as his wife, and compared unfavourably with Joseph, who refused to become involved with a foreign woman (43.5). Some characters are also said to be related when there is no basis for this claim in Scripture, such as the assertion that Goliath was David's cousin on their mothers' side (61.6).

The *Biblical Antiquities* is also characterized by detailed information about numbers and the names of people and places. The first chapter, for example, is made up entirely of genealogies, listing all of Israel's ancestors from Adam to Noah, including many people not named in Scripture, such as the later children of Adam (1.3) and the sons and daughters of Job (8.8). Some of these genealogies are based on Scripture, but may include more descendants, or give different names to a patriarch's wife and offspring. Other works of rewritten Bible, such as *Jubilees*, also show an interest in characters who are anonymous in Scripture, but some of the names used by Pseudo-Philo do not occur anywhere else in the extant Jewish literature. Such unique names include Seila for Jephthah's daughter (40.1), Eluma for Samson's mother (42.1), Sedecla for the witch of Endor (64.3), Bethac for the Levite of Judges 19 and Beel for the man who gave him hospitality.

Sometimes Pseudo-Philo locates an episode in a different place from the underlying scriptural narrative. Samson is said to have been locked up by the Philistines in the city of Ashdod, for instance, not Gaza (43.2; cf. Judg. 16.1–3), and the tribes of Israel gather to discuss the murder of the Levite's concubine at Shiloh, not Mizpah (45.5; cf. Judg. 20.1). It is not clear if there is any theological reason for these differences, or if the author simply made a mistake, or was drawing on a variant form of the scriptural text. The latter explanation is quite possible, as the earliest Greek translation of the Scriptures, called the Septuagint, occasionally disagrees with the Hebrew Bible over place names, and in these cases the *Biblical Antiquities* often follows the Septuagint; both, for example, locate the covenant renewal ceremony under Joshua at Shiloh rather than Shechem (*L.A.B.* 23.1; cf. Josh. 24.1). It may, however, be significant that several episodes are moved to Shiloh by Pseudo-Philo, perhaps indicating a desire to emphasize its importance in Israel's history (see also 22.1; 55.9).

The figures given in the *Biblical Antiquities* also frequently differ from the scriptural account and tend to be much higher. So, for example, the number of Philistines killed when Samson pulled down the pillars of his prison is said to be 40,000 (*L.A.B.* 43.8), rather than 3,000 (Judg. 16.27), and this text claims that around 45,000 Israelites were killed by the Benjaminites (*L.A.B.* 46.2–3), compared to the 22,000 mentioned in the report of this battle in the book of Judges (Judg. 20.21). Again, this may simply be a reflection of variant textual traditions, but it could also be a deliberate technique employed by the author to add drama to his narrative, or with the apologetic intent of making the ancient Israelites appear even stronger and more successful.

Other typical features of works of rewritten Bible are present in the *Biblical Antiquities* as well as in *Jubilees*, such as the addition of prayers and hymns spoken by leading characters at significant times, like on the eve of battle or death. Such prayers are attributed to, for example, Moses (12.8–9; 19.8–9), Joshua (21.2–6), Kenaz (27.7), Deborah (32.1–17) and David (59.4; 60.2–3), and are often loosely influenced by the Psalms (59.4). Pseudo-Philo also pays some attention to the emotions and inner motivation of scriptural figures. A good example of this is the scene he paints of the Israelites on the shore of the Red Sea after their exodus from Egypt, aware of the pursuing Egyptians at their back, urgently discussing their various options, whether to go back to slavery in Egypt, to throw themselves into the sea and die in that way, or to stand and fight (10.3). The thoughts of minor characters and of women in particular are brought to light, like Jael's trust in God as she prepares to kill Sisera (31.3–8; cf. Judg. 4.17–22) or Hannah's distress over the taunts of her rival wife Peninnah (50.1–5; cf. 1 Sam. 1.1–11).

As was also the case with *Jubilees*, there is some overlap with the genres of testament and apocalyptic: for example, fairly lengthy farewell speeches are created for Moses and Joshua (see 19.1–16; 23.1–14); Moses is said to have been shown by God some of the secrets of nature (19.10); and Kenaz receives a vision which appears to relate to the Creation and its ultimate transformation (28.7–9). Moses' revelation in particular includes echoes of apocalyptic-sounding language, with reference to the times being shortened and the light of the sun, moon and stars failing (19.12–15; see also 3.9–10; cf. e.g. Mark 13.14–27).

Finally, there are numerous examples within the *Biblical Antiquities* of the interpreter trying to answer questions raised by the underlying scriptural texts. He suggests, for instance, that Moses was not permitted to enter the promised land so that he would not have to endure the sight of the idols which the people of Israel would later worship there (19.7), and he explains that Korah was prompted to launch his rebellion against Moses by the pronouncement of the law about tasselled garments (16.1). Here the author is drawing an inference from the fact that in the narrative of the book of Numbers, the introduction of Korah follows on immediately from the statement of this law (Num. 15.37—16.3). The rabbinic interpreters also often make a direct connection, such as a causal link, between adjacent verses of Scripture, even when these do not appear on the surface to be about the same subject at all. Explanations are offered for other difficult passages, such as why the woman of Judges 19 should have been treated so brutally (she was a sinner, 45.3), or why God allowed Jephthah's own daughter to be the first one to meet him on his return from battle so that he had to offer her as a sacrifice (God did not approve of Jephthah's vow, since it could have resulted in the sacrifice of an unclean animal, 39.11). Contradictions in Scripture are also addressed, so that, for instance *L.A.B.* 61.9 states that an angel changed David's appearance after he slew Goliath, presumably to reconcile the disjunctures in the narrative of 1 Samuel chapters 16 and 17, where Saul seems to have forgotten who David is (1 Sam. 17.55–58), after having actually sent him to take on the Philistine (1 Sam. 17.31–39; cf. 1 Sam. 16.14–23).

Important themes in the *Biblical Antiquities*

God's faithfulness to the covenant made with the patriarchs is arguably the most important theological theme within the *Biblical Antiquities*. Speeches in particular are used to emphasize that the covenant will be maintained, however bleak the situation looks for the people of Israel. In an expansion of the biblical narrative, for example, Moses' father Amram is presented as urging his fellow-Hebrews to continue to bear children even when their newborn boys are being slaughtered in Egypt, because the covenant God established with Abraham, with its promise of many descendants, will surely be fulfilled (9.3–4). Good leaders are presented as particularly vocal in expressing their trust in God's ability to defend the people from danger because of his faithfulness to the covenant. Kenaz, for instance, reminds the Israelites on the eve of a battle against the Amorites of the mighty deeds that God has performed for them on account of the covenant (27.7). The giving of the covenant to Moses was solemnly witnessed by all the creatures of the world, and accompanied by dramatic signs such as lightning and earthquakes, according to *L.A.B.* 32.7–8.

One aspect of Pseudo-Philo's covenant theology is his frequently expressed hope that God's mercy will ultimately triumph over his justifiable anger at the people's sins (e.g. 19.11; 21.4; 22.5; 28.5; 35.3; 39.4–7; 49.3). God's ongoing care for and protection of the people of Israel is therefore stressed throughout the book:

> It is easier to take away the foundations and the topmost part of the earth and to extinguish the light of the sun and to darken the light of the moon than for anyone to uproot the planting of the Most Powerful or to destroy his vine. (18.10)

It is likely, then, that the author wrote partly to reassure his readers of God's continuing commitment to the covenant amid the political and social difficulties of their own day, and to motivate them to continue to hold fast to their traditional laws which he believed served to maintain this relationship. The *Biblical Antiquities* particularly encourages its audience to keep the sabbath, expanding the reference to this commandment in the account of the Decalogue (11.6–13; Exod. 20.1–17), for example.

Other behaviour strongly condemned as sinful includes idolatry and marriage to gentiles, which are frequently linked. Thus, in an addition to the biblical account unique to Pseudo-Philo, Tamar justifies her actions in seducing Judah with the explanation that having intercourse with her father-in-law was a less serious sin than marrying a gentile (9.5). In a catalogue of divine laws which have been broken by the Israelites (44.7) 'lust for foreign women' is listed as if it formed part of the Ten Commandments (for other examples of this theme, see also 30.1; 43.5; 44.7). Polemic against idol worship occurs frequently (e.g. 44.7; cf. 18.13; 39.6), so that the scriptural description of the people as 'doing what was evil in God's sight' is sometimes specified in the *Biblical Antiquities* as idolatry (see e.g. 41.3, cf. Judg. 13.11). This emphasis reveals something of the context in which the author was writing, as he clearly perceived a threat to Israel from the power of foreigners and the attractiveness of their religions. This theme of encouraging faithfulness to the law, especially to regulations which distinguish Israel from other nations such as those pertaining to the sabbath and to intermarriage, has already been identified above as being a key feature of *Jubilees* too.

Pseudo-Philo's understanding of the covenant as involving both an everlasting divine promise and the placing of demands on Israel in the form of the law has shaped his whole narrative. He rewrites the biblical material to make the point that breaking the commandments leads inevitably to punishment, and repentance to forgiveness: 'to every man there shall be such a punishment that in whatever sin he shall have sinned, in this he will be judged' (44.10). This outlook is often termed 'Deuteronomistic', as it also characterizes Deuteronomy and the biblical books which form the Deuteronomistic History, namely Joshua, Judges, 1 and 2 Samuel, and 1 and 2 Kings. This may partly explain the attention paid by the author to Israel's judges and early kings, since the underlying scriptural accounts of this period fit particularly well with this theological emphasis. Instances where this pattern appears to fail are, therefore, problematic for him and require explanation: in the case of Gideon, for example, who thrives despite his idolatry (e.g. Judg. 8.32), his punishment is said to be deferred until after his death (36.4).

The *Biblical Antiquities* reflects some of the other theological developments which are widely attested in Second Temple Jewish literature. So, as in many other writings of this time, including the *Book of Jubilees*, angels feature quite prominently in the narrative. Miriam experiences a dream-vision of an angel before the birth of Moses (9.10), for instance, and named angels help Kenaz to victory in a battle against the Amorites (27.10; for other examples of the appearance of angels where they are not mentioned in the corresponding account in Scripture, see 18.5; 19.12; 30.5; 32.1; 33.13; 34.2–3; 38.3; 61.5). A belief in guardian angels had evidently become well established by this time, judging by the specific references to them throughout the text (e.g. 11.12; 13.6; 15.5; 59.4; cf. *Jub.* 35.17). There is also one mention of the 'adversary', probably to be understood as a translation of the Hebrew *satan* (45.6). Echoes occur of aspects of the eschatological expectation set out in other contemporary writings, especially apocalypses such as *2 Baruch*. For example, Jonathan's words to David, 'even if death separates us, I know that our souls will know each other' (*L.A.B.* 62.9), parallel the view expressed elsewhere that the dead will recognize one another at the resurrection (cf. *2 Bar.* 50.3–4). A lengthy dialogue between God and Kenaz, which is not directly based on Scripture, may also illustrate the apparently widely held view that the Temple treasures would be hidden until the last day (26.12–15; cf. *2 Bar.* 6.4–10; *4 Bar.* 3.7–14; *T. Mos.* 1.17; 2 Macc. 2.4–8; Josephus, *Ant.* 18.4.1).

The rather more controversial theological question of whether the dead are able to intercede with God on behalf of the living also appears to be debated within the *Biblical Antiquities*, as it is in other writings of the time. One verse (33.5) clearly states that they cannot (cf. *2 Bar.* 85.12; *4 Ezra* 7.104–5), although the merits of Israel's ancestors *are* said to have helped in earning God's mercy for Israel in another passage (35.3; cf. 62.5 where David attributes the fact that he has not been captured by Saul partly to the righteousness of his father; cf. *T. Ab.* 14.8–14; 2 Macc. 8.15). Other early Jewish texts also witness to speculation about whether Moses actually died or was rather translated to heaven, a discussion prompted by the fact that the biblical account of his death states that his burial place is unknown, and implies that there were no witnesses to it (Deut. 34.5–6; see e.g. Josephus, *Ant.* 4.8.48; *T. Mos.* 1.15). Pseudo-Philo, therefore, seems concerned to emphasize the reality of Moses' death, and his burial by God (19.16).

Finally, the *Biblical Antiquities*, like *Jubilees*, reflects a high regard for the priesthood. One of the clearest examples of the esteem for priests which the author wishes to encourage is this comment by the significant character Kenaz about the priest Phinehas: 'Should anyone speak before the priest who guards the commandments of the Lord our God, especially since truth goes forth from his mouth and a shining light from his heart?' (28.3).

Other examples of rewritten Bible

There are two other important extant examples of early Jewish rewritten Bible, one by the first-century Jewish writer Josephus and another found among the Dead Sea Scrolls. The latter, called the Qumran *Genesis Apocryphon*, dates from either the first or second century BCE. Composed in Aramaic, it survives only in a single fragmentary copy. It rewrites the narratives about Noah and Abraham found in Genesis chapters 5—15. There is the expected blend of omission, expansion and rearrangement of scriptural material, and a concern to resolve perceived problems in the underlying narrative. For instance, an addition to the story of Abraham passing off his wife as his sister while in Egypt makes clear that Sarah remained unviolated because God prevented the pharaoh from actually approaching her for the whole time she was kept in his household (Gen. 12.10–20; *Genesis Apocryphon* 20.1–30). This work differs from other examples of rewritten Bible, however, in that parts of it are composed in the first-person rather than the third-person form, and it seems to be made up of different sections centring on the life of one of the patriarchs, which may have existed originally as separate sources. It is thus further removed from the scriptural text than *Jubilees* and *L.A.B.*, a distance increased by the fact that it is written in Aramaic rather than Hebrew. There is some relationship between the biblical interpretation preserved in the *Genesis Apocryphon* and the *Book of Jubilees*, but commentators remain divided about which is the earlier work, and whether one may have influenced the other.

The most extensive example of rewritten Bible known to us is Josephus' *Jewish Antiquities* (Books 1–11), which retells in Greek virtually the whole of the scriptural narrative. It is part of a longer work which goes on to recount the more recent history of the Jews right up until the author's own times, including the wars with Rome. This enormous undertaking was completed in 93–4 CE. Josephus follows the sequence of the biblical narrative closely, summarizing some sections and omitting a small number of episodes which he perhaps felt did not show the Jewish ancestors in a particularly favourable light, such as the Judah and Tamar incident (Gen. 38.1–30), Moses slaying an Egyptian (Exod. 2.11–12) and the making of the golden calf (Exod. 32.1–35). More frequently, however, Josephus expands the scriptural account with numerous interpretative and moralizing additions. These enable him to clarify ambiguities, explain difficult passages and answer questions which may have occurred to an educated contemporary reader, like why the patriarchs lived to such great ages. He also shapes his account to make theological points, such as stressing that disaster befalls those who do not keep God's laws.

It is generally accepted that Josephus had an apologetic motive in writing the *Antiquities*, seeking to familiarize his Graeco-Roman audience with Jewish history and religion, and to make it appear more accessible and attractive to them. He therefore uses language which his contemporaries would have understood, ascribing events to God's providence, for instance, and includes stylistic elements found in contemporary Greek novels and historical works. The most striking of these are the lengthy speeches he creates for several biblical characters, and his great interest in their underlying motivations and inner thoughts and emotions. These features are found to a lesser extent in *Jubilees* and Pseudo-Philo, but are far more developed and pervasive in the *Jewish Antiquities*.

The significance of the rewritten Bible texts

The significance of writings like *Jubilees* and the *Biblical Antiquities* for today lies in the light they throw on three main areas: the formation of the text of the Hebrew Bible, the tradition of early Jewish interpretation of it, and theological developments in the Second Temple period. First, these books sometimes seem to be reproducing a form of the scriptural text which is different from the Masoretic type which became the standard version in Judaism and which underlies the major modern translations of the Hebrew Bible. The dating used in the *Biblical Antiquities* often follows the Septuagint rather than the Masoretic text, for instance, as in *L.A.B.* 1.2, where Adam is said to have lived for 700 years after fathering Seth, in agreement with the Septuagint, where the Masoretic text has a figure of 800 years (Gen. 5.4; compare also Exod. 12.40 with *L.A.B.* 9.3). Similarities between the chronology of the Samaritan Pentateuch and the *Book of Jubilees* are also apparent, especially for the period between creation and the flood; both date the flood to the year 1307, for example (*Jub.* 5.22). The location of events in the *Biblical Antiquities* often varies from the standard Hebrew text: the placing of the covenant renewal ceremony under Joshua at Shiloh (*L.A.B.* 23.1; Josh. 24.1) rather than Shechem, as in the Septuagint, for instance, was noted above. A detailed examination of the wording of *Jubilees* and the *Biblical Antiquities* also reveals that both are sometimes closer to the Septuagint or Samaritan Pentateuch than to the Masoretic text: adultery comes before murder in Pseudo-Philo's list of the Ten Commandments and in the Septuagint account, for example (Exod. 20.13–14; *L.A.B.* 11.10–11). All this serves to illustrate that the form of the biblical text remained fluid to some extent for several centuries before an authoritative version was selected.

The rewritten Bible texts are also very important for the information they provide about the history of the early Jewish exegetical tradition, which has deeply influenced early Christian interpretation of the Bible. *Jubilees* is, for example, the oldest extant source for the claim that Moses wrote at least the book of Genesis and the first half of Exodus (*Jub.* 1.5). The *Biblical Antiquities* likewise sometimes provides an early witness to explanations which recur in later rabbinic texts, for example that Dinah was Job's wife (8.8), that Moses was born circumcised (9.13–15) and that the writing on the tablets of stone disappeared at the time of the golden calf incident (12.5). This interpretative tradition can be seen in the background of the New Testament, which was composed at a time very close to the *Biblical Antiquities.* It has been suggested, for instance, that the presentation of Jesus in the Gospels was coloured by developments in Jewish understanding of the offering of Isaac as having atoning value, even though his blood was not actually shed, because of his willing acceptance of a sacrificial death. Pseudo-Philo creates a speech, for example, in which God says: 'because he did not refuse, his offering was acceptable before me, and on account of his blood I chose them [i.e. the people of Israel]' (18.5; cf. 32.3; 40.2). A similar understanding of the sacrifice of Isaac is found in Josephus' *Jewish Antiquities* (1.13.2–4), *Targum Jonathan* on Genesis

22.12, and rabbinic sources such as *b. Yoma* 5a and *Mekilta de Rabbi Shimon* 4.

There are also interesting similarities between the accounts given in the *Biblical Antiquities* of the births of significant figures like Moses (9.9–10) and Samson (42.3–10) and the infancy narratives which open the Gospels of Matthew and Luke. These parallels illuminate the wider context of the New Testament presentation of Jesus as a new Moses, and of John the Baptist as a new Elijah or prophetic figure. *Jubilees* also uses some of the biblical passages which are important in early Christian literature, drawing on the book of Jeremiah, for instance, to assure the people that they will find God if they search with their whole heart (Jer. 29.13–14; *Jub.* 1.15; cf. Matt. 7.7–8), and echoing the promise of a new and everlasting covenant (Jer. 31.31–34; *Jub.* 1.18; cf. Heb. 8.7–12). As well as illustrating the development of interpretative traditions, these writings demonstrate the early origins of the exegetical techniques used by later Jewish and Christian commentators. Attention has been drawn above to some particularly clear examples of this, such as the way in which Pseudo-Philo's ability to make connections between different parts of the Bible prefigures the rabbinic method of *gezera shawa*, and his use of neighbouring scriptural passages to interpret one another, as in the identification of the law of the tassels as the cause of Korah's rebellion (16.1; cf. Num. 15.37—16.3).

Works of rewritten Bible provide further evidence of Jewish theology and thought in the Second Temple period, aspects of which are reflected also in the New Testament. Belief in angels, a final judgement and heaven and hell is widely attested in both *Jubilees* and the *Biblical Antiquities* (e.g. *Jub.* 2.2; 4.19; 15.27; 23.11; *L.A.B.* 18.5; 19.12; 32.9; 33.3, 13; 38.3; 61.5), for example, and the holy spirit also becomes more prominent, inspiring good leaders such as Kenaz and Deborah (*L.A.B.* 28.6; 32.14). The *Book of Jubilees* provides very early evidence for Jewish thinking about how festivals should be celebrated (e.g. Passover in 49.1–23) or how laws were interpreted in at least some circles of early Judaism. Its author also shared with some of the New Testament writers the view that the Torah was mediated through angels (*Jub.* 1.27; cf. Acts 7.53; Gal. 3.19; Heb. 2.2).

Finally, these texts raise important questions for adherents of Judaism and Christianity today about the status of Scripture and the acceptable limits of its interpretation. The authors of rewritten Bible clearly valued Scripture highly as the essential source of Jewish life and theology. However, they also apparently felt that the Scriptures required supplementation and even some rewriting, and they placed extrabiblical tradition on a par with Scripture itself, including both side by side and making no distinction between them. The Introduction to the *Book of Jubilees* makes this view particularly clear: it is implied that this work contains *all* the material which God revealed to Moses on Mount Sinai, not simply that which is recorded in the Pentateuch (e.g. *Jub.* 2.26). This form of writing may, then, cause modern believers to ponder how far they agree that traditions apart from Scripture should be regarded as authoritative, and how free contemporary religious leaders should feel to update the Scriptures for a new generation. *Jubilees*, the *Biblical Antiquities*, Josephus' *Jewish Antiquities* and other works like them raise the intriguing possibility of a new rewriting of the Bible to respond to contemporary insights or issues, such as those concerning feminism, sexual morality, global interdependence or human responsibility for the environment.

Further reading

Crawford, S. W., *Rewriting Scripture in Second Temple Times*. 2008, Grand Rapids, Michigan/Cambridge, UK: Eerdmans

Endres, J. C., *Biblical Interpretation in the Book of Jubilees*. 1987, Washington, DC: Catholic Biblical Association of America Press

Feldman, L. H., *Josephus's Interpretation of the Bible*. 1998, Berkeley: University of California Press

Halpern-Amaru, B., *The Empowerment of Women in the Book of Jubilees*. 1999, Leiden: Brill

Harrington, D. J., 'Pseudo-Philo'. In *The Old Testament Pseudepigrapha Vol. 2*. Ed. J. H. Charlesworth. 1985, New York: Doubleday, pp. 297–377

Murphy, F. J., *Pseudo-Philo: Rewriting the Bible*. 1993, New York/Oxford: Oxford University Press

Nickelsburg, G. W. E. and Collins, J. J. (eds), *Ideal Figures in Ancient Judaism*. 1980, Ann Arbor, Michigan: Scholars Press

Segal, M., *The Book of Jubilees: Rewritten Bible, Redaction, Ideology and Theology*. 2007, Leiden: Brill

Vanderkam, J. C., *The Book of Jubilees*. 2001, Sheffield: Sheffield Academic Press

3

Para-biblical literature or biblical expansions

Introducing the para-biblical literature

This chapter considers narrative texts which are linked in some way to the books which now comprise the Jewish Scriptures, either by being set in the context of a significant event in biblical history, such as the exile, or by being based loosely around a particular figure, like Joseph. A considerable number of such writings were produced by Jews living in the Diaspora throughout the Second Temple period, with some, the books of Tobit, Judith and Susanna, for example, being included in the Apocrypha. Works of this type differ from rewritten Scriptures in that they do not treat an extended section of the Bible, nor closely follow its sequence. Instead, they tend to concentrate on the lives of one or two main characters, quite often women, and they employ literary features such as extensive dialogue to provide entertainment as well as instruction for their audiences. Their authors sometimes imitate biblical forms and language in order to put across particular theological ideas or ethical teaching, but their plotlines generally have little basis in Scripture.

These narratives have been called 'biblical expansions', because they claim to tell their readers more about what happened to figures like Joseph or Adam. More recently, the term 'para-biblical literature' has come to be applied to them. This is not, however, a tightly defined literary genre, as these biblical expansions frequently incorporate other forms of writing, such as wisdom, apocalyptic or testaments. Their number and continued popularity witness to the centrality of the texts now called scriptural for Jewish identity and self-expression throughout this period, and also to the creativity with which inter-preters approached their authoritative texts.

Joseph and Aseneth

Introduction to *Joseph and Aseneth*

The starting point for *Joseph and Aseneth* is the scriptural narrative of Joseph's rise to prominence in Egypt. The author builds in particular on the brief reference in Genesis to his marriage to an Egyptian woman: 'And Pharaoh... gave him in marriage Asenath, the daughter of Potiphera priest of On' (Gen. 41.45). The story is told largely from the point of view of Aseneth, a rich and beautiful virgin who initially wants nothing to do with Joseph: 'an alien, and a fugitive... and was sold... the shepherd's son from the land of Canaan, and he himself was caught in the act, sleeping with his mistress...?' (4.9–10).[1] She is completely won over, however, as soon as she sets eyes on the handsome and powerful Joseph, so she undergoes a dramatic conversion to Judaism, which involves a mysterious encounter with an angel (14.1—17.10). She and Joseph are married (21.4–9), but before they can live happily ever after, she has to thwart a plot against them by Pharaoh's son and Joseph's brothers Dan and Gad (chapters 23—29).

Joseph and Aseneth, therefore, includes elements of different genres, since it both expands on Scripture and also reads like the kind of romantic novel popular in the Hellenistic world, such as *Cupid and Psyche*, *The Golden Ass* or *Chaereas and Callirhoe*. This demonstrates the ongoing interaction between Jewish and Graeco-Roman culture, and the willingness of Jewish authors to draw on popular literary forms; further examples of their engagement with poetry and drama will be seen in Chapter 4, below. The number of extant copies of *Joseph and Aseneth* which have been preserved in several languages, including Syriac, Armenian, Latin, Slavonic and Ethiopic, demonstrate that it continued to be attractive to Christian readers well into the mediaeval period.

The work's purpose, date and background are all difficult to establish with certainty. It has been preserved in both a long and a short form, with the majority of commentators regarding the longer version as the original; this fuller text will be considered here. There is no

---

[1] Translations of the texts in this chapter are taken from C. Burchard, 'Joseph and Aseneth' and M. D. Johnson, 'Life of Adam and Eve'. In *The Old Testament Pseudepigrapha Vol. 2*. Ed. J. H. Charlesworth. 1985, New York: Doubleday, pp. 177–247 and 249–95.

evidence about where or by whom it was composed, but an Egyptian provenance has been suggested, given that the narrative is set there. This is hardly conclusive, however, since it follows from the underlying scriptural location. It was written in Greek, in a style strongly influenced by the Septuagint, the Greek translation of the Scriptures. Although the oldest extant textual witness is a Syriac manuscript dating from the sixth century CE, the date of its original composition is usually put in the first century BCE or first century CE.

Joseph and Aseneth has long been understood as a Jewish work, dealing with the questions of conversion and intermarriage between Jews and gentiles, which were live issues for Diaspora Jews throughout the Second Temple period. However, more recently, its background has been questioned, because it is one of a number of writings transmitted by Christians with few features marking it out as obviously Jewish. The possibility of Christian authorship has therefore been advanced, since it makes no mention of the prescriptions of the Mosaic law, and it is quite conceivable that early Christians, too, had an interest in the subject of conversion from paganism. Some commentators find in the text possible references to the sacraments, especially the Eucharist, or suggest that it should be read as an allegory of the relationship between Christ and his bride the Church. Ross Kraemer, for instance, has made a detailed case for understanding *Joseph and Aseneth* as a Christian work dating from the late third or early fourth century CE.[2] However, the central issue of explaining the marriage of the biblical hero Joseph to a gentile, in contravention of biblical teaching, is likely to have been of greater concern to Jews than Christians, and an exalted picture of Jewish national heroes like Joseph and Jacob (22.7–8) is given throughout. Explicitly Christian themes are as rare in the text as Jewish motifs: any reference to baptism of the new convert, Aseneth, or to the role of Christ in bringing her to new life, for example, is entirely lacking.

It is most probable, then, that *Joseph and Aseneth* emerged within Jewish circles, and perhaps reflects contemporary discussion about the legitimacy of conversion and intermarriage, and the proper conditions for them. Its intended audience is likely to have been Jews, as familiarity with the Scriptures is assumed, but it may well

---

[2] R. S. Kraemer, *When Aseneth Met Joseph.* 1988, Oxford/New York: Oxford University Press.

also have served to encourage interested gentiles to follow the example of this prototypical proselyte, Aseneth, who is welcomed into the community of Israel on her conversion.

Key features of *Joseph and Aseneth*

Three features of *Joseph and Aseneth* are especially noteworthy: its relationship to the Scriptures; its similarities to the Hellenistic romantic novels; and its mystical dimension. The tale is ostensibly linked to the Joseph narratives recorded in Genesis. Thus the action commences in the first of the seven years of plenty (1.1; cf. Gen. 41.25–49), with Joseph depicted as actively gathering in the surplus grain at this time (1.2; 3.1). The arrival in Egypt of Jacob and his family during the seven years of the famine (22.1–2; cf. Gen. 42.1–5; 46.5—47.12) then forms the backdrop to the second part of the work. Dates are sometimes specified precisely, as in the books of *Jubilees* and *Biblical Antiquities* discussed in Chapter 2, above (e.g. 1.1–2; 22.1–2). Aseneth summarizes the story of Joseph's early years, recalling how he was sold into slavery, then was accused of sleeping with his master's wife and thrown into prison, only to be released because of his ability to interpret the pharaoh's dreams (4.9–10).

Joseph and Aseneth seeks to fill in two gaps in the scriptural account in particular: first, it provides additional detail about the power and status which Joseph enjoyed in Egypt, emphasizing the closeness of his relationship with the pharaoh, who was like a father to him (20.9), and explaining how he came to be ruler of the whole land of Egypt (cf. Gen. 45.8, 26). It is even stated here that Joseph reigned as king for 48 years after the pharaoh's death (29.9), a claim not made in Genesis but reflected elsewhere in early Jewish literature (e.g. Philo, *Joseph*, 120; *T. Levi* 13.9; *Targums Onkelos* and *Pseudo-Jonathan*). Second, it tells its readers far more than Scripture does about Joseph's wife Aseneth and about how they came to meet. The author thereby provides a solution to the problem raised by the marriage of Israel's great ancestor Joseph to a gentile woman, daughter of a pagan priest, a type of union expressly forbidden in numerous biblical passages. Jewish interpretative tradition deals with this difficulty in various ways, often, for example, identifying Aseneth as the half-Israelite daughter of Dinah and Shechem (Gen. 34.1–31;

cf. *Pirke de Rabbi Eliezer* 38; *Yalkut Genesis* 146). This view may be echoed in the second part of *Joseph and Aseneth*, where the biblical Shechem narrative is paralleled in Simeon and Levi's rescue of Aseneth from the sexual advances of a foreign prince (chapters 23—28). However, the main explanation offered here for this unlikely marriage is that Aseneth underwent a wholehearted conversion to Judaism before she married Joseph.

The question of the genre of *Joseph and Aseneth* has been extensively debated in recent decades. Richard Pervo,[3] for example, seeks to explain the text against the background of the romantic novels which were very popular in Graeco-Roman times. The heroines of these stories are usually, like Aseneth, beautiful virgins from the upper levels of society, whose gorgeous clothing and ornate chambers are described in detail (as in 2.1–12; 3.6). Their path to true love tends to be littered with adventures and obstacles, such as unrequited love, rival suitors or misunderstandings. Religion plays an important part in these novels, with the leading characters depicted as regularly offering prayers and sacrifices, and acknowledging the help of particular deities who intervene to protect them. The parallels with these ancient novels are not exact, as they are generally longer than *Joseph and Aseneth*, and include more adventures. However, this literary culture clearly influenced Jewish authors in the late Second Temple period, as is evident from other works such as Tobit and Esther; similar features have also been noted in early Christian accounts of female martyrs like Irene and Perpetua.

Even if *Joseph and Aseneth* cannot be classified as a novel in the full sense, then, it is important to recognize its skilful use of literary techniques such as lengthy dialogue and monologue, which enables the reader to really empathize with Aseneth's feelings, appreciating the depth of her sorrow for her old way of life (11.3—13.14; 21.11–21), for example, and the strength of her love for Joseph (6.1–8). The text includes a great deal of symbolism, such as colours (2.8; 3.6; 5.5), images of harvest, fruits and abundance (2.11–12; 4.1–2; 5.5), and a honeycomb full of bees (16.1–23), the meaning of which is not entirely clear, but which seems to represent life

---

[3] See e.g. R. I. Pervo, *Profit With Delight: The Literary Genre of the Acts of the Apostles.* 1987, Philadelphia: Fortress Press.

and immortality (16.16). Irony is also cleverly employed, as in the detail that Joseph assumes that Aseneth will want to press him to sleep with her (7.2–3), mirroring her recently expressed fears about his motives (4.10). The whole narrative is very carefully structured, so that, for instance, chapters 18—20 repeat the basic plot-line of chapters 3—8, but this time with the opposition between Joseph and Aseneth entirely removed, and first Joseph and then Aseneth appear dressed in royal attire, crowned and carrying a sceptre (5.4–5; 18.5–6; cf. 3.6).

Chapters 14—17 depict in detail an encounter between Aseneth and an angel, which serves to put an experience of divine revelation at the heart of *Joseph and Aseneth*. She is assured that her name is written in the book of life in heaven (15.4), addressed by a new name, 'City of Refuge' (15.7), and eats food which gives her a share in divine immortality:

> Behold, you have eaten bread of life, and drunk a cup of immortality, and been anointed with ointment of incorruptibility. Behold, from today your flesh (will) flourish like flowers of life from the ground of the Most High . . . and your youth will not see old age, and your beauty will not fail for ever. (16.16)

Following her angelophany, Aseneth's appearance is transformed so that she becomes 'like light, and her beauty was like heavenly beauty' (20.6). She is amazed at her own reflection (18.10), and similar awe and astonishment on seeing her is ascribed to her servant (18.11), Joseph (19.4–5) and her parents (20.6–7). This is an aspect of the narrative which is mystical rather than novelistic, and commentators have seen in it indications of a connection between this text and either the Graeco-Roman mystery religions or later Jewish *merkavah* mysticism.[4] The full meaning of these passages will be discussed further below, but they provide important evidence for the view that Second Temple Judaism was broader in its theology and ritual than is allowed for by some accounts of it which focus rather narrowly on groups about whom more is known, like the Pharisees and the Sadducees.

---

[4] See e.g. H. C. Kee, 'The Socio-Cultural Setting of Joseph and Aseneth'. *NTS* 29 (1983), pp. 394–413.

Important themes in *Joseph and Aseneth*

Joseph was a very popular subject for Jewish authors in the Diaspora, doubtless partly because he provided an example of an Israelite who had succeeded in acquiring wealth and influence in a gentile environment.[5] In *Joseph and Aseneth*, his power, status and virtue are all greatly enhanced. Joseph is strikingly handsome (6.4; 7.3; 13.14; cf. Gen. 39.6), completely chaste, merciful and meek (8.8), so that Aseneth's father Pentephres, for instance, describes him as 'god-fearing and self-controlled, and a virgin ... and ... also a man powerful in wisdom and experience' (4.7). He is presented as being totally loyal to the traditions of his people and religion, never eating with the Egyptians, for example (7.1, a reversal of the situation in Gen. 43.32 which reports that the Egyptians refused to eat with the Hebrews), and avoiding contact with gentile women in accordance with the instructions of his father Jacob (7.4–5; 8.5). The author may also have viewed him as a prophet, since 'nothing hidden escapes him, because of the great light that is inside him' (6.6), a description which matches Philo's statement that: 'To a prophet nothing is unknown, because he has intelligible light in him and shadowless rays' (*Spec.* 4.192). This may also be an allusion to the Egyptian name given to Joseph in Genesis 41.45, Zaphenath-paneah, which is interpreted as 'finder of hidden things' by Josephus (*Ant.* 2.6.1.91).

Joseph is called 'the powerful one of God' by both Aseneth and Pentephres (3.4; 4.7; 18.1; 21.21; cf.11.7), and his visit to their house is considered a great honour (2.2–4). Pentephres is himself a nobleman with an important position in society (1.3), but his response to Joseph's arrival is to prostrate himself before him (5.7) and to rejoice that the great man Joseph considered his household worthy of a visit (3.3). His standing is made clear in the detail that he rides through the land of Egypt on Pharaoh's second chariot, made of gold and drawn by pure white horses (5.4), and in the claim that Pharaoh himself is the only one who can fittingly preside at his wedding (20.8—21.8).

---

[5] The present author has surveyed the various treatments of the figure of Joseph in the literature of the Second Temple period; see S. E. Docherty, 'Joseph the Patriarch: Representations of Joseph'. In *Borders, Boundaries and the Bible*. Ed. M. O'Kane. 2002, Sheffield: Sheffield Academic Press, pp. 194–216.

That Joseph was king of Egypt is explicitly stated in the text (e.g. 4.7; 29.8–9), and in places he even appears to be depicted as a god. When Aseneth first sees Joseph, for example, he

> was dressed in an exquisite white tunic, and the robe which he had thrown around him was purple, made of linen interwoven with gold, and a golden crown (was) on his head, and around the crown were twelve chosen stones, and on top of the twelve stones were twelve golden rays. And a royal staff was in his left hand, and in his right hand he held outstretched an olive branch . . .   (5.5; cf. Gen. 41.42)

This description is reminiscent of traditional depictions of the sun god Helios, and an identification of Joseph with Helios might also be suggested by Aseneth's exclamation that: 'the sun from heaven has come to us on its chariot and entered our house today and shines in it like a light upon the earth' (6.2). That this aspect of Greek mythology did enter Jewish thought is indicated by some decorative floor mosaics from synagogues built in the early centuries CE which represent Yahweh as Helios in his heavenly chariot, clothed in white, purple and gold, and wearing a crown from which rays emanate. Joseph is certainly referred to throughout the text as a son of God (6.3, 5; 13.13; 18.11; 21.4), although commentators disagree about the exact significance of this phrase. Most take it as signalling that he is to be understood as God's representative, or as particularly close to God, rather than as an indication of his status as a divine redeemer figure.

Joseph and Aseneth is particularly interesting for what it reveals about the author's attitude to non-Jews. On the one hand, Aseneth needs to undergo a real and radical conversion from paganism in order to become a suitable wife for Joseph. He cannot even bring himself to kiss a woman who does not worship God (8.5), because idolatry results in death and destruction, as it is only the God of Israel who can give light, truth and life (8.9). Before she can be accepted by God, then, Aseneth needs to undertake a full week of serious repentance in which she dwells in isolation (10.2–17), smashes all her idols (10.12; cf. 13.11), puts on black mourning robes (10.8–10; cf. 13.3), fasts (10.1, 17; cf. 13.9; 15.3) and rolls on the floor in sackcloth and ashes (10.14–16; cf. 13.2, 4–7; 15.3). She is depicted as lamenting her sinful past at length (e.g. 12.4–6; 21.11–20) and is rightly hesitant about praying to God when she is defiled by a lifetime of worshipping idols (e.g. 11.7–8, 16–18). These actions and the week-long time frame perhaps symbolize the gravity of conversion, which cannot be brought about quickly or easily, because of the huge gap between the old way of life and the new.

On the other hand, the gentiles who appear in the story, including Pharaoh, appear as largely well disposed towards Joseph, and tolerant of his religious beliefs (4.7; 7.1; 9.1; 20.7; 21.4–6). Only Pharaoh's son is a real enemy of Joseph, and some Egyptians are described in particularly positive terms, with Pentephres, for example, said to be 'prudent and gentle, and . . . understanding' (1.5), attributes presumably thought fitting in the father-in-law of Joseph. Aseneth's prayers during her period of repentance imply that becoming a Jew could lead to ostracism by family and friends (11.4–6; 12.12), although in the narrative itself she faces no such difficulties, as her parents express only delight about her marriage to Joseph (e.g. 20.6–10).

It remains, then, a matter of debate as to how far this language reflects a contemporary situation in which Jews faced a lack of acceptance in Hellenistic society, and how far it should be read figuratively. Conversion to Judaism is, however, legitimized by the narrative: Joseph believes that proselytes can be numbered among God's people and inherit God's 'rest' or eternal life (8.9); Aseneth is readily embraced by Jacob as his daughter (22.8–10); it is said that she will become a shelter for other gentile converts (15.7; cf. Zech. 2.15); and she is protected by God in a time of danger (26.8; 27.10–11). Although welcomed, however, converts are not necessarily to be actively sought, since there is no suggestion that Aseneth's family should be urged to follow her example.

Belief in the existence of angels, and their activity on earth, is taken for granted in much of the literature of this period, and a central feature of *Joseph and Aseneth* is the appearance to Aseneth of a particularly magnificent angel (14.9) who can speak on behalf of God (15.3–8). Since he describes himself as 'chief of the house of the Lord and commander of the whole host of the Most High' (14.8), it is often assumed that he should be identified with Michael, the archangel who features in other early Jewish and Christian writings, but he explicitly refuses to reveal his name to Aseneth

(15.12). Interestingly, another female angel is introduced (15.7–8), called Repentance, who is the guardian of all virgins and has a special care for Aseneth. She should possibly be understood as an angelic counterpart of Aseneth (15.7–8) or as the heavenly representation of the human virtue. Similar ideas are found in other sources; so, for example, the angel Phanuel is said to be set over all actions of repentance in *1 Enoch* (*1 En.* 40.9). Angels are presented here as being able to eat (16.15; cf. 15.14–15, but contrast e.g. *T. Ab.* 4.9–10) and to interact with each other like humans (15.7–8; 16.12–14).

The theme in *Joseph and Aseneth* which has perhaps attracted the most attention from commentators is the repeated refrain that the one who worships the true God 'will eat blessed bread of life and drink a blessed cup of immortality and anoint himself with blessed ointment of incorruptibility' (8.5; cf. 8.9; 15.4; 16.16; 19.5; 21.21). Various suggestions have been put forward to try to explain what is meant by these references to life-giving food, drink and ointment. Some argue that they are evidence of a fusion of synagogue worship and mystery religions, in which sacred meals played an important part, or that they allude to Jewish ritual meals, such as those eaten by communities like the Essenes or the Therapeutae; nothing else in the text fits with the practices of these groups, however, which promoted celibacy rather than celebrating marriage, and did not advocate the wearing of finery like Aseneth's. Others see in them a reference to the eucharistic bread and wine and to the anointing of baptism. This would indicate a Christian origin for the text, or at least Christian interpolation, something which is not certain, although there are notable similarities between these verses of *Joseph and Aseneth* and some New Testament passages (e.g. John 6.35, 48; 1 Cor. 10.14–22).

The most common view, however, is that this triad of bread, wine and oil stands for the whole of Jewish life, as it does in several scriptural passages (see e.g. Ezra 3.7; Pss. 23.5; 104.15; Dan. 10.3; Hos. 2.8, 22; cf. Judith 10.5; 1QH 10.24; *Apoc. Ab.* 9.7), so refers to the everyday actions of pious Jews, who eat kosher food and use oil in the ways prescribed by the purity laws. A significant theological claim is thus being made, namely that the Jewish religion confers life and immortality on its adherents.

The episode in which the angel gives a miraculous honeycomb to Aseneth to eat (16.1—17.4) has prompted similar debate among scholars, since this honeycomb also apparently symbolizes or even brings about eternal life (16.16). It is variously interpreted as a metaphor for the Jewish law (cf. e.g. Pss. 19.10; 119.103; Philo, *Fug.* 137–9), or as an allusion to the manna given to the Israelites in the wilderness which tasted like honey (Exod. 16.31). Marc Philonenko associates it with the Egyptian goddess Neith, whose name Aseneth bears, and one of whose symbols was the bee.[6] Since honey was often fed to newborn infants in ancient societies, the passage has also been seen as a possible allusion to an initiation rite in which the convert is being reborn into a new way of life. Such rituals were an important part of the practices of the Graeco-Roman mystery religions like the cult of Isis, but there is little surviving evidence about the form they took. The honeycomb is perhaps best understood, therefore, as signifying that the bread, wine and oil of which Aseneth will partake after her conversion is really the food of angels, in which faithful Jews already share on earth:

> this comb is (full of the) spirit of life ... And all the angels of God eat of it and all the chosen of God and all the sons of the Most High, because this is a comb of life, and everyone who eats of it will not die for ever and ever ...
>
> (16.14)

The belief that those who worshipped the true God were already in some respects living an angelic life is found in some of the Qumran *Thanksgiving Hymns* (1QH), and perhaps also in the *Testament of Job* (*T. Job* 48.2—50.2; see below, Chapter 5) and early Christian writings such as the Epistle to the Hebrews (e.g. Heb. 12.18–29).

One commentator, Gideon Bohak, finds in this scene the key to understanding the purpose and origins of *Joseph and Aseneth* as a whole. He argues that the book is an allegory written to justify the founding of a Jewish temple in Egypt (as referred to in e.g. 1 Macc. 4.34; *1 En.* 90.8; Dan. 9.26; 11.22; Josephus, *Ant.* 12.237; 13.73; *J.W.* 1.31–3). The bees which come out from the honeycomb and settle on Aseneth's lips and on fruit trees near her house are in his opinion

---

[6] M. Philonenko, *Joseph et Aséneth: Introduction, texte critique, traduction et notes.* 1968, Leiden: Brill.

symbolic representations of the temple priests, who wear garments the same colours as these bees (Exod. 28.4–5), and who have left their homes in Jerusalem and built a new temple in Heliopolis, the very city where Aseneth dwells. Aseneth's house is depicted as being like a temple, with springs and fruit trees in the courtyard (2.10–12), and a private inner sanctuary (2.7–9).[7] This is certainly an innovative theory, and one which takes seriously the honeycomb scene, which is obviously important to the narrative but which remains opaque to modern readers. However, the author of *Joseph and Aseneth* was remarkably subtle if he did indeed intend the narrative to serve as a legitimization of the Egyptian Jewish temple, since there are no other obvious references to this, and the main theme of the story appears to be Aseneth's conversion. This proposal also demands a relatively early date for the text's composition, soon after the founding of the temple at Heliopolis in the mid-second century BCE; this seems unlikely given the author's indebtedness to the language of the Septuagint, which was only being completed at that time.

One aspect of the narrative of *Joseph and Aseneth* which might offer some support to Bohak's explanation of its background is the prominence in the second part of the narrative of Levi, the ancestor of the priestly families:

> And Aseneth loved Levi exceedingly beyond all of Joseph's brethren, because he was one who attached himself to the Lord, and he was a prudent man and a prophet of the Most High and sharp-sighted with his eyes, and he used to see letters written in heaven by the finger of God and he knew the unspeakable mysteries of the Most High God and revealed them to Aseneth in secret. (22.13; cf. 23.8; 26.6)

His role in the destruction of Shechem is highlighted (23.12; cf. Gen. 34.1–31), and on this similar occasion when a female member of his family is in danger, it is Levi who perceives this first and rushes to help Aseneth (26.6; cf. 28.15–17). He, together with Simeon, refuses to take part in the plot to attack Joseph, spurning the inducements of money, property and rank offered by Pharaoh's son, and standing up to his threats (23.3–4), and at the end of the story it is he who advocates forgiveness (29.3–4).

---

[7] G. Bohak, *Joseph and Aseneth and the Jewish Temple in Heliopolis*. 1996, Atlanta: Scholars Press.

Levi is often depicted particularly positively in literature emanating from priestly circles, such as *Jubilees* or the *Testament of Levi*, and it is also common in Second Temple Jewish literature to see Joseph's brothers treated differently, as in the *Testaments of the Twelve Patriarchs*, for example (discussed further below, in Chapter 5). So here, the real villains are said to be Dan and Gad: all the blame for selling Joseph into slavery is attributed to them (24.9; 25.6; 28.13), and they are depicted as motivated by envy of Joseph and Aseneth (22.11; 24.2) to join the pharaoh's son in plotting against them. Benjamin, on the other hand, is praised as exceptionally beautiful, strong and godfearing (27.1), and he also plays a key role in rescuing Aseneth, by knocking Pharaoh's son off his horse with a stone and severely wounding him (27.2–5), a part of the narrative which is clearly modelled on the biblical story of David and Goliath.

The author echoes the theology of numerous Hellenistic Jewish writers in emphasizing that Joseph's God is the life-giving Creator, in contrast to the lifeless and dumb idols of Egyptian religion (8.3, 9; 12.1–2). The text also makes reference to God's mercy and compassion (11.10, 18), and fatherly care for those in particular need, such as orphans or the persecuted (11.13; 12.6–14; 13.1). There is no mention of God's role in Israel's history or the giving of the law, but Aseneth's prayers reveal a strong sense that God is a constant source of 'refuge' for those who turn to him (11.3, 11; 12.3, 6, 13; 13.1, 12). The main ethical teaching of the story is that those who truly worship God will not repay evil for evil (23.9; 28.5, 14; 29.3) or injure others (23.11). Aseneth and Levi put this teaching into practice, for example, by showing forgiveness to Dan and Gad (28.10; 29.3–4). Aseneth also describes her earthly riches as transient, unlike the gifts of God which are everlasting (12.15), demonstrating that the idea of leaving behind worldly goods in order to gain something better in heaven is not found only in the New Testament (e.g. Mark 10.29–30), but is part of wider Jewish tradition (cf. e.g. *T. Job* 18.6–8; see further below, Chapter 5).

The Life of Adam and Eve

Introduction to *The Life of Adam and Eve*

The Life of Adam and Eve exists in several versions and languages, including Greek, Latin, Armenian, Georgian and Slavonic. These all overlap in content to some extent, but also exhibit considerable differences from one another. Their starting point is the scriptural account of the expulsion of Adam and Eve from the Garden of Eden after they eat the fruit of the forbidden tree (Gen. 3.1–24). The work was probably written originally in Greek, and it seems that subsequent translators felt free to adapt it, or to incorporate into it additional traditions which were also in circulation. This suggests a lively ongoing interest in the stories of Adam and Eve and in the effects of their disobedience on all humankind, as evidenced also in later Christian art and literature, such as the paintings of the Renaissance artists and Milton's *Paradise Lost.*

In order to distinguish the two main forms of the text, the Greek and the Latin, from one another, this chapter will follow scholarly convention and use the abbreviated title *Life* for the former and *Vita* for the latter. The Greek *Life* is the shortest of the extant versions, and is largely an expanded retelling of the events of Genesis chapter 3. Adam and Eve are pictured recounting this story in turn to their extended family, who have gathered together around Adam's deathbed. Their words serve to explain to their children the necessity of illness and death, and to warn them of the serious consequences of disobeying God's commandments. Yet the narrative also holds out the prospect of divine mercy and life after death for all humankind, since it goes on to relate how, on his death, Adam is forgiven and taken up to join God and the angels in heaven (see especially *Life* 37).

The Latin version follows the same basic outline as the Greek and includes Adam's account of the fall, but not Eve's longer retelling of these events. However, it contains additional material, most notably a speech in which Satan explains that he was expelled from heaven because he refused to join the other angels in worshipping Adam as the image of God (*Vita* 12.1—16.3). This legend is reflected in several other sources, including *2 Enoch* (29.4; 31.3), some mediaeval Christian writings and the Qur'an. The *Vita* also dwells at greater length on a section of the narrative which describes Adam and Eve voluntarily undertaking a harsh penance of standing up to their necks in the cold waters of the Rivers Tigris (Eve) and Jordan (Adam) for many days in order to persuade God to take pity on them and provide them with the food of which they have been deprived since being cast out of the garden (*Vita* 4.1—6.3). Eve is said to have been deceived by Satan for a second time during this ordeal (*Vita* 9.1—10.4; cf. *Life* 29.15–17). The Armenian and Georgian versions contain much of the material present in both the Greek and Latin forms.

It is not at all certain whether *The Life of Adam and Eve* should be treated as a Jewish work, because some versions and sections of it were evidently composed by early Christians. It has long been thought that an originally Jewish writing underlies the current forms of the text, hence the decision to include it in this volume, but this view is increasingly being questioned in scholarly research. Robert Kraft and James Davila are among those who have argued most persuasively for a rethinking of the traditional assumption that any pseudepigraphon which is not obviously Christian must be Jewish in its origins.[8] The main argument in favour of a Jewish basis for *The Life of Adam and Eve* is the lack of mention of Jesus' role in saving humanity from sin and death, which seems inexplicable in an early Christian work about Adam in the light of New Testament passages like Romans 5.12–14. However, there are no specifically Jewish references either, such as to Moses or the commandments of the Torah, and all the extant manuscripts were produced and transmitted by Christians in the mediaeval period. Most commentators today, therefore, incline to the view that all forms of the text should be regarded as early Christian compositions, which may perhaps incorporate pre-existing Jewish traditions.

It is difficult to date any of the versions of *The Life of Adam and Eve* precisely, partly because there are no unambiguous historical references within the narratives, so they are generally assigned to the period between the second and fourth centuries CE. It is certainly clear from sources like Paul's letters and the writings of church fathers such as Irenaeus that early Christians were as interested as their Jewish contemporaries in what the early chapters of Genesis might teach about sin, forgiveness and the human condition. The complexities around this question of provenance will doubtless continue to be a significant aspect of future study of the literature of the Second Temple period, and it is an important reminder of the shared roots of the two religions of Judaism and Christianity.

---

[8] See e.g. R. A. Kraft, 'The Pseudepigrapha in Christianity'. In *Tracing the Threads: Studies in the Vitality of Jewish Pseudepigrapha.* Ed. J. C. Reeves. 1994, Atlanta: Scholars Press, pp. 55–86; and J. R. Davila, *The Provenance of the Pseudepigrapha: Jewish, Christian or Other?* 2005, Leiden: Brill.

Key features of *The Life of Adam and Eve*

The Life of Adam and Eve in all its forms can be classified as an example of 'biblical expansion' or 'para-biblical' writing because it is clearly based on a scriptural narrative, but goes far beyond it. Thus it expands the account of the banishment of Adam and Eve from the garden given in Genesis chapter 3 with great detail, including speeches, prayers, explanations of the actions of the main characters, and comment on their thoughts and inner emotions. Adam is pictured begging God for forgiveness and the chance to remain in paradise (*Life* 27.1–3), for example, and the devil discloses that the underlying reason for his determination to deceive and harm the first humans is the fact that he blames them for his own expulsion from heaven (*Vita* 11.1; 16.3).

The texts also seek to develop a wider story about the lives of Adam and Eve after the fall, considering, for instance, how they managed to find food outside the garden (*Life* 1.1—2.2; 29.7; *Vita* 1.1—2.3; 22.1); how they responded to the murder of their son Abel by his brother Cain (*Life* 2.1—4.2; *Vita* 23.1—24.2); how they dealt with illness (*Life* 9.1—13.2; *Vita* 35.1—43.2); and what happened to them when they died (*Life* 32.4—42.3; *Vita* 45.1—48.3). Some of these traditions clearly arise from an attentive reading of Genesis chapter 3, which does raise such questions, and clarification is offered in the Greek *Life* of another controversial verse, Genesis 3.7: 'Then the eyes of both were opened, and they knew that they were naked.' Taken literally, this sentence might be read as implying that Adam and Eve were born physically blind, and the implication that they walked around constantly naked before the fall was also problematic for some later exegetes, so a metaphorical interpretation of it is offered here, as in other Jewish texts: 'And that very moment my eyes were opened and I knew that I was naked of the righteousness with which I had been clothed' (*Life* 20.1; cf. Philo, *QG*, 1.39–40).

The narrative does not follow a straightforward chronological format, but is told predominantly in the form of extended flashbacks as Adam prepares for his death. This feature illustrates the difficulty of categorizing texts satisfactorily, since, in this respect, *The Life of Adam and Eve* closely resembles the genre of testament, or farewell speech, which will be discussed below in Chapter 5. The Greek version differs from the usual testament format, however, in that the longest speech is given not by the person who is actually dying, but by Eve as Adam's death approaches (*Life* 14.3—30.1). There is also some overlap with the genre of apocalyptic (see Chapter 6, below), most notably in the account of Adam being taken up to heaven (*Vita* 25.1—28.2) and Eve's vision of God enthroned (*Life* 33.1—36.3).

Important themes in *The Life of Adam and Eve*

Texts which have as their scriptural point of departure Genesis chapter 3 will naturally be concerned with the question of the origins of sin and suffering. *The Life of Adam and Eve* is in line with the main currents of Jewish and Christian theology in attributing responsibility for this to Adam, Eve and the serpent, avoiding any suggestion that God is the creator of evil. Adam is, therefore, accused of breaking God's commandment and listening to his wife (*Life* 24.1; 39.1; *Vita* 34.1), Eve of listening to the serpent and ignoring the commandment (*Life* 25.1; cf. *Vita* 18.1), and the serpent of acting as an instrument of Satan and leading astray the unwary humans (*Life* 26.1; cf. 16.5). The Greek *Life* in particular expands on the rather bald account of Genesis, picturing the main actors hesitating before committing their sin, asking further questions about it and expressing their fear of God's anger at their disobedience (*Life* 16.4; 18.2; 21.4).

The culpability of Adam and Eve is stressed in all versions of the text, then, and Eve is even said to have been tricked a second time by the devil in the disguise of an angel so that she abandoned a period of penance early, believing God had already forgiven her and Adam (*Life* 29.15–17; *Vita* 9.1—10.4). However, the authors also go to some lengths to explain the actions of the first humans, which has the effect of mitigating their wrongdoing. Eve is temporarily left alone in her part of paradise by the angels who usually guard her there, for example, allowing Satan the opportunity to sneak in and seduce her (*Life* 7.2; 17.1; *Vita* 33.1–3). The close link established between Satan and the serpent whose actions he directs (*Life* 16.1–5; 17.4; 26.1; cf. *Vita* 9.1; 11.2) also serves to imply a diabolical origin for sin, somewhat weakening human responsibility. This connection is not made in Genesis, but is common in later interpretation (see e.g. Rev. 12.9; 20.2).

Plenty of space is given to describing the sincere repentance of Adam and especially of Eve, thereby painting a more sympathetic and rounded picture of them (*Life* 9.1–2; 10.2; 14.3; 27.2; 29.11–14; 32.1–3; *Vita* 1.1; 3.1; 4.3—8.2; 11.1; 18.1–3; 35.2–3; 44.5), and the narratives also assert that both are ultimately forgiven and gain eternal life (*Life* chapters 36—43; *Vita* chapters 45—48). The part played by Eve in these texts has attracted the particular interest of commentators. Her guilt is emphasized above Adam's in the Latin version (e.g. *Vita* 3.2; 18.1; 33.3; 35.3; 44.2–5), but less so in the Greek *Life*, where she speaks at greater length than Adam, and is the one who gives the farewell testament in place of her dying husband. John Levison has argued that Eve is presented more positively in chapters 15—30 of the Greek *Life* than elsewhere in the work, or in the Latin *Vita*, so this section may have been an originally separate account of the fall, which existed in either oral or written form and was then incorporated into the larger story of *The Life of Adam and Eve*.[9] Whether or not this is the case, it is striking that Eve is given such a prominent role in *The Life*, is afforded the opportunity to explain her actions and is granted a heavenly vision. This is a further example of the interest in women characters which is a noteworthy feature of biblical expansions and also of other early Jewish writings, such as the rewritten Scriptures (as discussed above, in Chapter 2).

The Life of Adam and Eve, particularly in the Greek version, is concerned at least as much with the related question of death and the afterlife as with the origins of human sin. This is suggested both by the form of the text, which is presented in part as the last words of the dying Adam and his wife, and also by the detailed attention paid to describing Adam's burial (*Life* 37.3—42.3). It is not surprising that later readers of Genesis came to wonder about the ultimate fate of Adam and Eve, and whether they were ever reconciled with God and given a share in the resurrection. The view of this literature is that, while death is an unavoidable consequence of the fall for Adam (see e.g. *Life* 28.4), and by implication for every human being, it is very definitely not the last word because God has promised life after death: 'I told you [Adam] that you are dust and to dust you

---

[9] J. R. Levison, 'The Exoneration of Eve in the Apocalypse of Moses 15—30'. *JSJ* 20 (1989), pp. 135–50.

shall return. Now I promise to you the resurrection; I shall raise you on the last day in the resurrection with every one of your seed' (*Life* 41.3; cf. 28.4). This sends a very powerful message of hope to the readers, who need not doubt the certainty of receiving God's mercy and future blessings, since even those thought to be responsible for bringing sin and death into the world are granted eternal life.

The detailed description of funerary rites in the final part of the *Life* may provide some evidence about the background of the text's authors. This section is thought by some scholars to indicate a Christian origin for the work, or at least considerable Christian interpolation, since it includes an account of Adam being washed three times by a seraph in the lake of Acheron immediately after his death (*Life* 37.3). This was a ritual for cleansing the dead from their guilt known from Greek literature (e.g. Plato, *Phaedo* 113 a, d) and referred to in early Christian writings (e.g. *Apocalypse of Paul* 22; *Sib. Or.* 2.338). It may also be an allusion to Christian baptism, which sometimes took the form of three immersions in water, reflecting the three persons of the Trinity, especially as Adam's tomb is said to have been sealed with a triangular seal (*Life* 42.1), another possibly Trinitarian symbol.

The picture given in *The Life of Adam and Eve* of the human condition is that the devil is a constant threat to everyone. He is termed 'the enemy' throughout the Greek *Life* (2.4; 7.2; 15.1; 25.4; cf. *Vita* 12.1; 33.2), and perhaps the story of his second deception of Eve (*Life* 29.15–17; *Vita* 9.1—10.4) is meant to symbolize that his efforts at temptation are ongoing after the fall. The narratives function, therefore, as a lesson to their audiences about the consequences of disobeying God, a warning made explicit in the last words of Eve's farewell speech in the *Life*: 'Now then, my children, I have shown you the way in which we were deceived. But you watch yourselves so that you do not forsake the good' (*Life* 30.1). Exactly what 'not forsaking the good' or acting properly consists of is nowhere spelled out, though, and specific ethical injunctions are lacking, apart from one reference to covetousness or desire as the origin of every sin (*Life* 19.3; cf. Rom. 7.7; Jas. 1.15).

However, the text also places considerable emphasis on human beings as having been made in the image of God. It is this status which the devil blames for his own loss of heavenly glory in the

Vita (13.1—16.3) and which protects Eve and Seth from an attack by animals: 'And the beast said to Seth, "See, I stand back from the presence of the image of God, as you have said"' (*Vita* 39.3; cf. *Life* 12.2). In the *Life* (33.5) the angels are also depicted as begging God to forgive Adam because he is made in God's own image. Since Adam and his descendants all bear this divine likeness, they will ultimately be restored to the bliss they enjoyed in the garden and to immortality (*Life* 28.4), and will rule over the devil (*Life* 39.3; *Vita* 47.3). The eschatological picture is not worked out in any great detail, but there are several descriptions of the heavens (see especially *Life* 33.1—37.6; *Vita* 25.1—29.3): Adam is brought to the third heaven when he dies (*Life* 37.5; cf. 2 Cor. 12.2), for instance. The important role of numerous ranks of angels is taken for granted throughout both the *Life* and the *Vita*, with special prominence given to the archangel Michael (*Life* 3.2–3; 13.2–6; 22.1; 37.4–6; 38.1; 40.1–4; 43.1–3; *Vita* 13.3—15.2; 21.2; 25.2; 29.1–3; 41.1–3; 45.1; 46.3; 48.1–3; 51.2).

A further theme of *The Life of Adam and Eve* is an interest in sickness and medicine. In both the Latin and Greek versions, Adam's children ask him about pain and illness (*Life* 5.5; *Vita* 30.4; 31.5), and the many diseases which now afflict people are explained as an inescapable punishment for the first sin (*Life* 8.2; *Vita* 34.1–3). Eve and Seth embark on a quest for healing oil to ease Adam's suffering (*Life* 9.3—13.2; *Vita* 36.1—42.1), for example, but are unsuccessful because illness has become an inevitable part of human life: the angel Michael tells Seth: 'you are by no means able to take from it, except in the last days' (*Vita* 42.1; cf. *Life* 13.2). This idea of Seth undertaking a journey to retrieve the oil of mercy from paradise continued to be popular in later mediaeval Christian literature. His character plays a far greater role throughout *The Life of Adam and Eve* than in the book of Genesis: apart from this episode, his birth is particularly celebrated as providing a replacement for the murdered Abel (*Life* 4.1–2; *Vita* 24.1–2); he acts as the spokesperson for all Adam's descendants as they gather around his deathbed (*Life* 5.4); he offers to travel to the gates of paradise to beg God for some of its produce to bring back to his father (*Life* 6.1–3; *Vita* 31.1–4); he shares in the heavenly visions of both Adam (*Vita* 25.1—29.3) and Eve (*Life* 34.1—36.3); and he writes down the story of Adam and Eve and other special knowledge which has been transmitted to him on stone tablets to be read by later generations (*Vita* 51.3–9). It is interesting to note how often the para-biblical writings take a particular interest in minor scriptural characters such as Seth and Aseneth as a vehicle for developing new aspects of the biblical narrative.

Other examples of biblical expansion

Several examples of biblical expansion are included within the collection of deutero-canonical or apocryphal books, notably Tobit, Judith and Susanna. In all of these narratives, piety and obedience to the commandments and Israelite tradition is encouraged, Jewish–gentile relations are often at issue, and an important place is given to women characters. Their common message is that those who remain faithful to God, even in difficult and dangerous circumstances, will be protected, whether individuals like Susanna who was falsely accused of adultery, or the whole people of Israel, delivered from the threat of the Assyrian armies by the hand of Judith.

Early Christians continued this practice of composing works loosely connected to the Scriptures, sometimes drawing on existing Jewish sources or interpretative traditions. As explained above, this was probably the case with *The Life of Adam and Eve*, and a further example of this is the *Ascension of Isaiah*. This text falls into two parts, beginning (chapters 1—5) with the story of how the biblical prophet Isaiah met his death by being sawn in half by King Manasseh (5.1; cf. Heb. 11.37). Some scholars, for example Michael Knibb,[10] think it likely that these chapters have taken over an existing Jewish work on the martyrdom of Isaiah, but an increasing number of commentators now doubt this, preferring rather to read the whole of the *Ascension of Isaiah* as an early Christian text dating from the second century CE. Certainly it is difficult to separate out any underlying Jewish source from its current Christian frame, since even this first section includes prophecies about the coming of Christ and the life of the Church (3.13—4.22). Chapters 6—11 then report an

---

[10] See e.g. M. A. Knibb, 'Martyrdom and Ascension of Isaiah'. In *The Old Testament Pseudepigrapha Vol. 2*. Ed. J. H. Charlesworth. 1985, New York: Doubleday, pp. 143–76.

apocalyptic experience of Isaiah, in which he journeys through the seven heavens and learns in advance about the descent of God's Messiah or 'beloved' to earth, and his death, resurrection and return to heaven.

The *Ascension of Isaiah* is particularly interesting for what it reveals about Christianity in the early second century, a period from which relatively few other written sources have survived. Contemporary debates about the humanity and divinity of Christ and the relationships within the Trinity are reflected here, for instance (see e.g. 9.40; 11.7–20), and perceived dangers to the Church identified, such as the spread of false teaching and leaders concerned only for their own gain (3.21–31; cf. 1 Tim. 3.1–13; 6.3–10; 2 Pet. 2.1–3). The *Ascension of Isaiah*, and the developing traditions about Adam and Eve, then, illustrate the persistence of this genre of para-biblical literature within early Christianity as well as early Judaism.

The significance of the para-biblical texts

Like the rewritten Scripture texts discussed in Chapter 2, above, the narratives considered in this chapter are extremely significant for what they reveal about the development of theological thinking and biblical exegesis in the Second Temple period. *The Life of Adam and Eve*, for example, wrestles with important questions which continue to exercise Jews and Christians today, such as the origins of sin and death, the extent of human responsibility for it, the depths of God's forgiveness and the nature of life after death. Its message about the certainty of divine mercy and the significance for human beings of their creation 'in God's image' is one theological response to these issues which can continue to provoke reflection and inspire hope. *Joseph and Aseneth* likewise puts forward interesting theological views, such as the possibility that God's faithful people can share in angelic life while still on earth.

Just as significant as the content of the para-biblical works, however, are the literary forms chosen as the vehicle for putting across the authors' views. The similarities between narratives like *Joseph and Aseneth* and the ancient Hellenistic romantic novels in particular suggest that the need to entertain as well as edify the audience was well understood. The use of these literary genres also indicates that many Jews were embedded in the wider culture in which they operated, influenced by it and open to what it had to offer, and further examples of this point will be discussed in Chapter 4, below. These writings can be viewed, then, as early examples of the attempt to 'inculturate' Jewish theology and engage with the contemporary world, and so offer a particular perspective on an issue which continues to be a matter of debate within several of the world's religions.

The para-biblical texts highlight some of the scriptural passages which caused difficulty for later interpreters, such as Joseph's marriage to the daughter of an Egyptian priest, for instance, or the idea of the pre-fall nakedness of Adam and Eve. They also witness to the development of exegetical traditions which recur in later writings, as in the linking of the serpent with Satan in *The Life of Adam and Eve* (*Life* 16.1–5; 17.4; 26.1; cf. *Vita* 9.1; 11.2; cf. Rev. 12.9; 20.2), and the understanding of God's 'rest' as eternal life in *Joseph and Aseneth* (*Jos. Asen.* 8.9; cf. Heb. 4.1–11). In addition, they illustrate how minor scriptural figures like Seth or Joseph's brothers Dan and Gad were viewed in later interpretation. Women characters in particular are the subject of interest and enhancement, with Aseneth becoming something of a heroine, for example, and even Eve perhaps being partially exonerated for her role in the fall.

Works of this genre reveal something important about the understanding of Scripture itself among the communities who wrote them: their authors and readers clearly experienced no difficulty in accepting the idea that the biblical narratives could be expanded or serve as the jumping-off point for other stories. For these Jews and Christians, Scripture was considered to be authoritative divine revelation, but it was nevertheless open to further reflection. It naturally prompted new interpretations and innovative theological developments, since its relevance to all generations and circumstances had constantly to be drawn out. Indeed, the need to ensure its ongoing application was a more important task than reproducing its fixed words.

Finally, these texts are important test-cases for those scholars like James Davila and Robert Kraft who have been at the forefront of research into the provenance of the Pseudepigrapha. For they show clearly the connections between early Judaism and early Christianity, in that it is hard to ascribe definite Jewish or Christian origins to many of these para-biblical works. The overlap, for instance, between the ethical ideals of the New Testament and *Joseph and Aseneth*, with its stress on showing mercy to enemies and putting heavenly reward above earthly goods, is striking, as is the use in both of the imagery of the bread of eternal life. All this provides students of early Christianity with essential information about the wider context of the New Testament and of the Judaism from which it emerged. It is particularly important to appreciate that these writings witness to the diversity of early post-biblical Judaism and, like the Qumran discoveries, offer a glimpse of a Second Temple Judaism which was far broader in its theology, attitudes and forms of worship than has often been supposed.

Further reading

Chesnutt, R. D., *From Death to Life: Conversion in Joseph and Aseneth.* 1995, Sheffield: Sheffield Academic Press

Davila, J. R., *The Provenance of the Pseudepigrapha: Jewish, Christian or Other?* 2005, Leiden: Brill

Humphrey, E. M., *Joseph and Aseneth.* 2000, Sheffield: Sheffield Academic Press

Knight, J., *The Ascension of Isaiah.* 1995, Sheffield: Sheffield Academic Press

Stone, M. E., *A History of the Literature of Adam and Eve.* 1992, Atlanta: Scholars Press

4

Non-narrative literature:
poems, hymns and drama

Introducing the non-narrative literature

Several writings from the Second Temple period make use of forms other than narrative. These texts were inspired by both contemporary Graeco-Roman poetry and biblical models like the Psalms. They were written for a variety of intended audiences and purposes, enabling their authors to express their own fears and hopes for the future, for example, and to educate others about Jewish history, beliefs and ethical values. This chapter will consider three significant extant examples of this non-narrative literature, representing the Judaism of both Palestine and the Diaspora, and covering an interesting range of genres.

The *Exagoge* of Ezekiel the Tragedian

Introduction to the *Exagoge*

The *Exagoge* is a drama, written in Greek in the second century BCE, which recounts in verse the story of the exodus. Its author sought, therefore, to retell the Jewish Scriptures through the medium of a literary form which was shaped by Greek poets such as Aeschylus and Euripides. It is significant for both theologians and classical scholars because it is the only surviving example of this type of writing by a Jewish author, and is also the longest extant Greek tragedy or drama. The full text has not been preserved, but fortunately we have access to it through the lengthy quotations of the later Christian writers Clement of Alexandria (*Stromateis* 1.23.155–6) and Eusebius (*Praeparatio Evangelica* 9.28–9), who reproduced 269 lines of the *Exagoge*, probably around a quarter of the original.

Nothing is known of the author, such as whether Ezekiel was his own name or a pseudonym, or if he composed any further plays or poems on biblical themes which have not come down to us. Evidence for the activity of any other Jewish dramatists at this time is very limited, although the roughly contemporary *Letter of Aristeas* (*Let. Aris.* 312–16) does refer negatively to Greek poets trying to include passages from the Scriptures in their works. Ezekiel is often assumed to have lived in the Egyptian city of Alexandria, but it is impossible to claim with certainty any more than that he was a Diaspora Jew, steeped in Graeco-Roman culture and literature. His play was probably intended to both educate and inspire a Jewish audience, and to explain Jewish history and customs for gentiles, and persuade them of the greatness and special qualities of his people.

The *Exagoge* is usually divided by commentators into five acts, as was the standard pattern in Greek drama, comprising:

- a long opening speech by Moses, followed by his meeting with the seven maidens including his future wife, called here Sepporah;
- a dream by Moses of a heavenly throne, interpreted by his father-in-law;
- an encounter and dialogue between Moses and God at the burning bush;
- a speech by an Egyptian messenger recounting the crossing of the Red Sea;
- a report by Israelite scouts on the oasis at Elim.

The work therefore follows the narrative of Exodus chapters 1—15 very closely, but introduces non-scriptural material in two places, in Moses' dream, and in the final scene at Elim, where a magnificent bird, probably a phoenix, is said to appear. A chorus may also have played a part in responding to certain scenes. There is some debate about whether the *Exagoge* was meant to be actually performed in a theatre or was composed as a purely literary work, with the majority of recent commentators, including Howard Jacobson, arguing strongly that it was written to be enacted on stage.[1]

Key features of the *Exagoge*

The *Exagoge* is written entirely in verse, in the iambic pentameter form. A sense of this literary style can be gained from reading Robertson's translation of the opening lines, spoken by Moses:

---

[1] See H. Jacobson, *The Exagoge of Ezekiel*. 1983, Cambridge: Cambridge University Press.

> And when from Canaan Jacob did depart,
> With threescore souls and ten he did go down
> To Egypt's land; and there he did beget
> A host of people: suffering, oppressed,
> Ill-treated even to this very day
> By ruling powers and by wicked men.
> For King Pharaoh, seeing how our race increased
> In swarms, devised against us this grand scheme:
> He forced the men to manufacture bricks
> For use in building lofty walls and towers;
> Thus with their toil he made his cities strong.
> He ordered next the Hebrew race to cast
> Their infant boys into the river deep.[2]   (lines 1–13)

As these verses suggest, all the important elements of the Exodus narrative are included in the play, and the author generally follows the biblical account closely, but, as in the rewritten Scripture genre discussed above in Chapter 2, some incidents are expanded, while others are summarized or passed over. The institution of the Passover is explained at considerable length in two speeches (lines 152–93), for example, but there is no mention of the people's rebellion at Marah (Exod. 15.22–26).

Some differences from the scriptural original are dictated by the dramatic structure of the *Exagoge*. For instance, it would have been technically problematic to depict the ten plagues on stage, so these have to be presented in the form of a speech by God foretelling what will befall the Egyptians (lines 132–51). This has the effect of truncating the time span of Exodus chapters 7—8. Similarly, since the crossing of the Red Sea and the drowning of the Egyptians would also have been difficult to enact, Ezekiel introduces a lone Egyptian survivor who can report fully on these events (lines 193–242). Such messengers bringing eyewitness reports of battles play a frequent role in Greek drama, featuring in Aeschylus' play *The Persians*, for example.

The *Exagoge* is an important witness to some early exegetical traditions about Moses, such as his royal education (lines 36–8; cf. Philo,

---

[2] Unless otherwise stated, all translations of the text are taken from R. G. Robertson, 'Ezekiel the Tragedian'. In *The Old Testament Pseudepigrapha Vol. 2*. Ed. J. H. Charlesworth. 1985, New York: Doubleday, pp. 807–19. Robertson aims for a metrical translation of the text; a rather more literal, but less poetic, rendering can be found in Jacobson, *Exagoge of Ezekiel*, pp. 50–67.

Moses 1.20; Acts 7.22), especially those which provide answers to perceived difficulties in the scriptural narrative. For instance, it is not clear from the early chapters of the book of Exodus quite how the young Moses came to know that he was Jewish, but this text explains that his mother taught him all about his ancestral race and religion while nursing him (lines 34–5). Significantly, it is also stated here that when the Hebrew people left Egypt, their wives were given jewellery and clothes by the local women as compensation for all the work they had done there (lines 162–6), so they did not solicit or plunder these goods as implied in Exodus (Exod. 12.35–36). Other Jewish sources also seek to justify this action on the part of the departing Hebrews, perhaps responding to gentile accusations of theft (e.g. *Jub.* 48.18; Philo, *Moses* 1.41–2; Josephus, *Ant.* 2.314; *b. Sanh.* 91a).

Moses flees to Libya rather than the land of Midian in the *Exagoge*, and Libya is described here as the home of the Ethiopians (lines 60–5; cf. Exod. 2.15–18). This identification may have been prompted by a desire to reconcile Moses' marriage to Zipporah in Midian (Exod. 2.16–21) with the reference elsewhere in Scripture to his Ethiopian wife (Num. 12.1). Several plagues which in the biblical account affect both humans and animals are limited in the *Exagoge* to humans – the boils, the pestilence and the death of the firstborn (lines 132–48; cf. Exod. 7.1—8.32; Ps. 78.50 apparently employs a similar exegetical tradition). Furthermore, the plague of the pestilence is said to be directed only at the hard-hearted (line 140), and the killing of the firstborn is linked to the sin of arrogance (line 148). Such additions may have been introduced to explain or mitigate the extreme harshness of God's treatment of the Egyptians. Various other non-scriptural details included here are present in other early Jewish writings or in rabbinic literature, such as Moses striking the Red Sea with his staff in order to part its waters (lines 224–8; cf. *L.A.B.* 10.5; Philo, *Moses* 1.177; Josephus, *Ant.* 2.338; cf. Exod. 14.21) and the figure of one million drowned Egyptians (line 203; cf. *Jub.* 48.14).

Important themes in the *Exagoge*

Some caution must be exercised in attempting to draw out significant theological themes from the *Exagoge*, since the surviving text is incomplete. Nevertheless, it is possible to comment on the ways in which Ezekiel subtly enhances the figure of Moses, who literally takes centre-stage in this work, and on his particular presentation of the people of Israel. First, some emphasis is placed on the fact that Moses himself decided to leave the Egyptian court:

> But when I grew into an adult,
> I went forth from the royal palace at my spirit's urging,
> To see the deeds and devices wrought by the king . . .
>   (lines 39–41, Jacobson's translation)

The interpretation that Moses made a conscious choice to leave the comforts of Pharaoh's palace and identify with the suffering Hebrews is found elsewhere in early Jewish sources, and is reflected also in the New Testament: 'By faith, Moses, when he was grown up, refused to be called the son of Pharaoh's daughter, choosing rather to share ill-treatment with the people of God than to enjoy the fleeting pleasures of sin' (Heb. 11.24–25).

The account in the *Exagoge* of the way Moses intervened on the second occasion when he came across two men fighting may also hint more strongly than the underlying scriptural narrative at his future role as defender of the oppressed and powerless. Thus he does not ask the aggressor why he is beating his fellow-Hebrew, as in Exodus 2.13, but rather why he is striking a weaker man (line 50). Finally, the objections Moses raises when God commissions him to go to the king to ask for the release of the Hebrews are conflated and summarized here (lines 113–15; cf. Exod. 4.1–14), and any reference to God's angry response to these complaints (Exod. 4.14) is omitted entirely. This reduces the focus on an aspect of the Exodus account which casts Moses in a more negative light, as hesitant and unwilling to obey God.

The inclusion of a vision of a heavenly throne (lines 68–89) is a particularly important key to understanding Ezekiel's portrayal of Moses. In this dream, Moses sees an enormous throne on the top of Mount Sinai, on which sits a royal figure, presumably God, who then invites him to sit down on it and gives him the symbols of kingship: a crown and a sceptre. Moses is able to survey the whole earth and the heavens, and even the stars do homage to him. The vision is interpreted as a prediction that Moses will become a great king and will have prophetic powers, seeing things in the past, present and future. Dreams were frequently used in Greek drama to introduce ideas or events which could not be easily presented on stage, and they are an equally common motif in Scripture: this passage, for example, echoes Joseph's dreams of his future exalted position (Gen. 37.7–9) and Daniel's vision of the Ancient of Days (Dan. 7.13–14).

There is some disagreement among commentators about exactly what the throne-vision indicates about the author's view of Moses. Pieter van der Horst, for instance, argues that Moses is presented here as a divine being, and that these verses are an early example of the kind of mystical speculation which characterizes the later Jewish *merkavah* literature.[3] Howard Jacobson, on the other hand, plays down the mystical or supernatural aspects of this scene, finding significance in the fact that Moses' encounter with God is said to be an imaginary or visionary one, not a real ascension and conversation in heaven.[4] There is no doubt, however, that this vision serves to emphasize Moses' uniquely close relationship with God, and to present him as both a king and a prophet. This depiction goes beyond the biblical text, but similar traditions about Moses are reflected elsewhere in early Jewish sources (e.g. Philo, *Moses* 1.148–9), perhaps inspired by the account of his mysterious encounter with God on Mount Sinai in Exodus 24, or the final chapters of the book of Deuteronomy in which he is said to relate the future of Israel (Deut. 31—33).

As well as giving this enhanced picture of Moses, the author of the *Exagoge* tends to present the ancient Israelites in a more positive light than the scriptural narrative does. There is no mention, for example, of any possibility that they might refuse to listen to Moses (Exod. 4.1; 6.9), nor of their complaints about the lack of water at Marah (Exod. 15.22–25). Similarly the people do not rail bitterly against Moses for encouraging them to leave the safety of Egypt when they see the pharaoh's army pursuing them (lines 204–12; cf. Exod. 14.10–12).

The author may also have been concerned to emphasize the theme of God's care for the Hebrews. The weakness of their plight at the

---

[3] See P. van der Horst, 'Moses' Throne Vision in Ezekiel the Dramatist'. *JJS* 24 (1983), pp. 21–9.
[4] H. Jacobson, 'Mysticism and Apocalyptic in Ezekiel the Tragedian'. *Illinois Classical Studies* 6 (1981), pp. 272–93.

Red Sea is highlighted, for instance, in the statement that they were unarmed and had women and children to care for, in contrast to the ordered, well-equipped Egyptian forces (lines 193–219). Nor does the text as it stands make clear that the Israelites faced a long and arduous journey from Egypt to Canaan, an aspect of the scriptural account which might detract from a picture of both God's powerful control of events and concern for the people. However, this point cannot be established with certainty, since the whole play is not extant, and may originally have included reference to such matters. It is perhaps significant, though, that the description of the first resting place to which God led the Hebrews, the oasis at Elim, does go beyond the Exodus narrative in elaborating on its beauty and suitability as a camp. In language perhaps influenced by Hellenistic ideas of utopia, the *Exagoge* speaks of a lush and shady meadow which provides fruitful trees and good pasture for the flocks (lines 243–53).

Interestingly, there is also an account of the appearance of a fabulous bird at Elim (lines 254–69). This creature is not identified in what remains of the text, but these verses fit well with other ancient descriptions of the phoenix bird, and are cited as a description of it by a later source, Pseudo-Eustathius. In Graeco-Roman literature, utopia is often described as populated by birds, both common and extraordinary ones, and sightings of the phoenix were thought to happen only very rarely, marking especially momentous events. Its appearance at Elim may, therefore, be intended to heighten the sense of the significance of the exodus events, and its association with this site may also have been suggested by the fact that the Greek term for palm trees used in the Septuagint translation of Exodus 15.27 is the same word, *phoinix*.

The *Exagoge* is particularly important for the light it sheds on relationships between Diaspora Jews and their gentile neighbours in the second century BCE. Ezekiel's use of the dramatic genre is in itself evidence that at least some Jews were well educated in Hellenistic language and culture and perfectly at home in it, and he has, for example, no difficulty in attributing the ability to interpret Moses' dream to a non-Jew (lines 83–9). The very fact that he expected an audience for his work is also an indication of a prevailing mood of openness: it suggests both that Jews were positive about retelling their Scriptures in Greek forms, and that gentiles would have been sufficiently interested in Jewish history to read or attend a play based on the theme of the exodus.

The text may also hint at certain areas of sensitivity, in that the lengthy explanation of the Passover (lines 153–92) includes no reference to the specific restriction of this festival to those who are circumcised (Exod. 12.43–44), perhaps because both the custom of circumcision and the perceived Jewish tendency to social exclusivity were criticized by many gentiles. It is also noteworthy that the author prefers the term 'Hebrews' to 'Jews' or 'Israelites'. Possibly he simply felt that this was a more accurate or historically appropriate designation for the people of the exodus generation, but it may also stem from a reluctance to link contemporary Jews living in the Diaspora too closely to the land of Judaea, a fairly insignificant and sometimes rebellious region. The whole emphasis of the play as we have it is on the escape from the place of persecution, not on the final destination, which is never named as the land of Israel, nor described in the glowing terms found in Scripture. Overall, Ezekiel's *Exagoge* seems to reflect a place and a period in which relationships between Jews and gentiles were largely positive, and in which a Jew educated in Greek culture could be sufficiently confident about his religious identity to attempt this retelling of the exodus events through the medium of a thoroughly Hellenistic literary genre.

The *Psalms of Solomon*

Introduction to the *Psalms of Solomon*

The *Psalms of Solomon* is a collection of 18 hymns written by an unknown group of Palestinian Jews in the mid to late first century BCE. Jerusalem has often been proposed as the specific setting for its composition, as a number of the psalms (see especially 2, 8, 17) allude directly and vividly to events taking place there, and Jerusalem is personified as the speaker or addressee in others (e.g. 1, 11). These historical references are used by commentators to help date the psalms, and they appear to reflect the turbulent times between approximately 80 and 30 BCE. The community of devout Jews behind these poems were vehemently opposed to the Israelite rulers of the time, the Hasmonaeans, regarding them as corrupt, violaters of the Temple cult, and illegitimate because they were not descended from the line of David. This Hasmonaean dynasty was eventually over-thrown by Roman invasion, and two of the psalms in particular describe the advent of a foreign ruler in terms which best fit what is known of the Roman general Pompey.

According to Josephus' account of this period (*Ant.* 14; cf. *Pss. Sol.* 8.14–22), Pompey was initially welcomed by some of the Jewish people and their leaders when he marched on Jerusalem in 63 BCE, but then encountered resistance from other factions based in the Temple, so that a civil war and a siege lasting several months ensued, during which the city's inhabitants endured great hardships and many lost their lives. Pompey was ultimately victorious, and entered the Temple with his troops, desecrating it (see *Pss. Sol.* 2.2). Some years later (48 BCE) he was assassinated in Egypt, and did not receive a proper burial (see e.g. *Pss. Sol.* 2.25–7).[5] In seeking to reflect on these events in the form of hymns, the *Psalms of Solomon* stands in the tradition of the biblical book of Lamentations, a series of poems composed in response to an earlier national catastrophe, the Babylonian exile in 587 BCE.

The original language of these psalms is generally thought to be Hebrew, but they have survived only in translation, in a small number of Greek and Syriac manuscripts, most of which date from no earlier than the tenth century CE. There is evidence that they were read and transmitted by early Christians, and were even sometimes included as part of their Scriptures: the fifth-century Codex Alexandrinus, for example, has a heading for the *Psalms of Solomon* after the books of the Old and New Testaments and the letters of Clement, although the actual leaves which would have contained the text are missing. They are also joined in some manuscripts to the early Christian collection of hymns known as the *Odes of Solomon*, suggesting that they may later have come to be used in the liturgy of the Syriac Christian Church.

The individual hymns which make up the collection of the *Psalms of Solomon* were almost certainly written by more than one person

---

[5] Commentators are largely agreed that Pompey is the foreign ruler alluded to in *Pss. Sol.* 2, 8 and 17, but a case has been advanced for understanding 'the lawless one' of *Pss. Sol.* 17.11ff. as a reference not to Pompey but to Herod the Great; see K. Atkinson, 'Toward a Redating of the Psalms of Solomon: Implications for Understanding the *Sitz im Leben* of an Unknown Jewish Sect'. *JSP* 17 (1998), pp. 95–112.

over a period of time, although they reflect similar concerns and views. It is quite probable that they were used in worship by members of the circle in which they were produced. Their original purpose may also have been at least partly didactic, as several offer a theological explanation of contemporary disasters as God's punishment on sinners (e.g. 2.3–33; 8.4–23; 9.1–3; 15.10–12; 17.5–25). Their association with Solomon may have been prompted by the belief that he wrote many songs (1 Kings 4.32), or because of his biblical reputation as the kind of wise and righteous Davidic king for whom the authors longed.

Until around the middle of the twentieth century, most commentators linked the *Psalms of Solomon* with Pharisaical circles, because of the emphasis the hymns place on piety and the law (e.g. 3.8; 14.2–3); their views about fate and the balance between divine control of events and individual responsibility (5.4–6; 9.4–5; cf. Josephus' description of the Pharisees in *Ant.* 13.5.172–3; *J.W.* 2.8.163–5); the distinction which is frequently drawn between the righteous person and the sinner; the opposition expressed towards the Hasmonaean dynasty (see especially 1, 8, 17); and the fact that they attest to a belief in resurrection (3.12). These are all positions thought to be characteristic of the Pharisees, but in fact many other Jews of the time shared these beliefs and attitudes, and there may even have been some overlap of membership between the different religious parties.

The discovery of the Dead Sea Scrolls has also prompted a re-evaluation of the question of the provenance of the *Psalms of Solomon*. In general terms, these Qumran texts highlight the diversity of Judaism in the late Second Temple period, and several of them also offer interesting specific parallels to these hymns in areas such as messianic expectation, or in the hostility voiced towards the Jerusalem priests and leaders. These similarities do not mean that the *Psalms of Solomon* should now be associated with the Qumran community rather than with the Pharisees, but rather they illustrate the complexity involved in seeking to attribute any early Jewish writing to one particular, identifiable group.

Key features of the *Psalms of Solomon*

There are obvious correspondences in form, style and content between the *Psalms of Solomon* and the canonical book of Psalms which doubtless served as its inspiration. Thus, individual hymns of differing lengths and dates have been gathered together, and given brief titles, such as 'A Psalm of Solomon' (1, 5), or 'A Psalm of Solomon Concerning the Righteous' (3). Some common topics are treated, such as the contrast between the righteous and the wicked person, or God's concern for the poor and the persecuted. Several of the main genres found among the scriptural psalms can be identified here also, such as individual and community laments (see e.g. 7.1–10; 16.6–15), and thanksgiving songs (15.1–6; 16.1–5). God is frequently addressed directly, in praise or entreaty, and several prayers or hopes are framed in the first person singular, for example:

> When I was persecuted I called on the Lord's name;
> I expected the help of Jacob's God and I was saved . . .
> (15.1)[6]

The biblical Psalm 72, which is entitled 'A Psalm of Solomon', may have served as a particular model for *Psalms of Solomon* 17, with its description of a righteous king who will be widely honoured by foreign nations and will care for the needy within Israel.

These hymns also draw extensively on the imagery and language of a wide range of other scriptural books. The indictment of the arrogance of the Roman general Pompey in *Psalms of Solomon* 2 echoes the condemnation of the prince of Tyre in Ezekiel 28.1–10, for instance, and the description of the contemporary plight of Jerusalem in the same psalm reflects a passage in Isaiah:

> She put on sackcloth instead of beautiful clothes,
> A rope around her head instead of a crown.
> She took off the wreath of glory which God had put on her;
> In dishonour her beauty was thrown to the ground.
> (2.20–21; cf. Isa. 3.24)

Two of the hymns also offer interesting interpretations of the text from Isaiah about making a straight highway for God in the wilderness (Isa. 40.3–4), which is applied in the New Testament to John the Baptist (Matt. 3.3; Mark 1.3; Luke 3.4–6; John 1.23): one psalm

---

[6] All translations of the text are taken from R. B. Wright, 'Psalms of Solomon'. In *The Old Testament Pseudepigrapha Vol. 2*. Ed. J. H. Charlesworth. 1985, New York: Doubleday, pp. 639–70.

looks forward to the time when God will level the ground to enable exiled Jews to return to Jerusalem (11.2–6; see also Isa. 60.4), but another sees it as a reference to Israel's leaders, who smoothed the way for Pompey's entrance into the city (8.16–17).[7] There are also parallels between *Psalms of Solomon* 11 and a number of other eschatological hymns composed in the Second Temple period, especially Baruch 5.5–8, to which it may be related literarily, or with which it may share a common source (cf. also Tobit 13.10–18; Sir. 36.1–17).

Important themes in the *Psalms of Solomon*

The *Psalms of Solomon* offers some significant theological reflections on a tumultuous period of Israel's history. Particular hymns (see 2, 4, 8, 17) comment critically on the secular and religious leaders of the first century BCE, both the native Hasmonaean kings and the Roman invaders. Sometimes these rulers are condemned in general terms, but on occasion specific individuals appear to be in view. It is not always a straightforward matter to identify these figures, however, since the psalms do not supply any actual names, but instead make use of cryptic designations like 'the sinner' (2.1), 'the dragon' (2.25), 'the profaner' (4.1) or 'the lawless one' (17.11). Such coded allusions are a feature of several apocalyptic writings (see further Chapter 6, below) and of some of the Qumran texts, which refer to the enemies of their community as 'the wicked priest' and 'the man of lies', for example, and to the Romans as the 'Kittim' (see especially 1QpHab, e.g. II.12; III.4; IV.5; VI.1; VI.10; IX.7).

There is debate among commentators as to whether this practice reflects a real fear of persecution or is simply a literary convention. It should be noted, however, that the criticism of contemporary leaders in the *Psalms of Solomon* is trenchant and hardly veiled, which suggests either that the hymns circulated only within a very tight group or that those who used them did not expect to be punished for their views. One of the main concerns of the authors of these psalms was the conduct of Temple worship, which they considered had been defiled through the behaviour of the contemporary priestly leadership and the general sinfulness of the people:

---

[7] A full exploration of the use of the Scriptures in this work is to be found in K. Atkinson, *An Intertextual Study of the Psalms of Solomon.* 2000, Lewiston, New York: Edwin Mellen Press.

> Their lawless actions surpassed the gentiles before them;
> They completely profaned the sanctuary of the Lord.
>
> > (1.8; cf. 2.3; 8.12)

It is evident from a variety of sources that this issue of Temple purity was a very contentious one in the first century BCE, and it is possible that this group, like the Qumran community, had separated themselves from the Jerusalem cult due to disagreements over principles and practice. Other sins of which the leaders and people in general are accused here include sexual immorality, hypocrisy, arrogance, excessive wealth, lying and slander (see especially 1.4–8; 2.11–13; 4.1–5; 5.16; 8.9–12; 12.1–3).

This political and religious context of the *Psalms of Solomon* undoubtedly accounts for some of its theological emphases, particularly the theme of God's judgement which pervades the whole collection. As in many scriptural texts (including canonical psalms such as Ps. 28), the disasters befalling the people of Israel are understood as divine punishment for sin:

> For you have rewarded the sinners according to their actions,
> And according to their extremely wicked sins . . .
>
> > (2.16; cf. 2.3–10; 8.4–22; 17.5–10)

The suffering of the members of the authors' own group has also to be explained, however, since they did not consider themselves guilty of wrongdoing. In an interesting theological move, therefore, a number of hymns distinguish between God's just punishment of the wicked and the fatherly discipline with which he cleanses the righteous. This theme is particularly noticeable in *Psalms of Solomon* 10, 13 and 14, and is clearly expressed in these lines:

> For the discipline of the righteous (for things done) in ignorance
> Is not the same as the destruction of sinners . . .
> For he will admonish the righteous as a beloved son
> And his discipline is as for a firstborn . . .
>
> > (13.7–9; cf. 3.4; 7.3; 8.26; 10.1–3; 14.1; 16.11, 13)

The devout are therefore urged to respond appropriately to God's chastening by accepting it and repenting of any sins which they may have committed, either deliberately or unknowingly (see e.g. 10.1; 16.11), in order to receive God's mercy (16.15; cf. 13.10–11; 15.13).

The *Psalms of Solomon* does, then, stress God's mercy as well as righteous judgement (see e.g. 2.35–6; 4.25; 5.15; 6.6; 10.6–8; 11.1; 13.12; 14.10). This message would have been important for strengthening the community's resolve in the difficult circumstances which it faced, and it also reflects the pattern of sin–repentance–forgiveness–salvation which is put forward in several scriptural texts, especially the books of the Deuteronomistic History. The ninth hymn, for example, reflects on the Babylonian exile, attributing this disaster to the transgressions of the people of that time, but ending with an assurance of God's everlasting mercy towards the house of Israel. This hope is grounded in the theology of the covenant, in which these psalmists continue to believe, in spite of the disparity between their present experience and the covenant promises:

> For you chose the descendants of Abraham above all the nations,
> And you put your name upon us, Lord,
> And it will not cease forever.
> You made a covenant with our ancestors concerning us,
> And we hope in you. (9.9–10; cf. 18.1–3)

Such encouragement to trust in an unbreakable bond between God and Israel is an important aspect of the theology of several of the writings considered in this volume, especially those composed in Palestine in the particularly turbulent period around the turn of the era, such as the *Biblical Antiquities* and *4 Ezra.*

Connected with the emphasis on God's judgement is the distinction drawn in several of these psalms between the behaviour and ultimate fate of 'sinners' and the 'righteous' or 'devout':

> May the wicked perish once and for all from before the Lord.
> And may the Lord's devout inherit the Lord's promises.
> (12.6; cf. e.g. 2.33–37; 3.3–12; 4.8; 13.11; 14.1–10; 15.4–13)

The righteous are assured of God's protective care (e.g. 3.5–6; 4.23; 5.2–14; 6.1–6; 7.7; 8.31; 12.5; 13.1–4; 16.4) and can look forward to eternal life (3.12; cf. 14.10), while the wicked will face destruction and eternal darkness in Hades (12.6; 15.10; cf. 3.11; 14.9). This division of humanity into two camps is particularly evident in *Psalms of Solomon* 15, which suggests that those who will receive

God's salvation are distinguishable from those destined for death by
the presence of a visible sign:

> For God's mark is on the righteous for salvation . . .
> But . . . those who act lawlessly shall not escape the
>   Lord's judgement . . .
> For on their forehead (is) the mark of destruction . . .
>
>   (15.6–9)

This motif may be an echo of biblical texts, like the mark put on Cain
to protect him from being murdered (Gen. 4.15), or the sign in
blood on the Israelites' doors ensuring that the plague of death would
pass over their houses at the time of the exodus (Exod. 12.13, 22–23;
cf. Ezek. 9.6; Rev. 7.3; 14.9).

The repeated contrast between the 'righteous' and the 'wicked'
is a prominent feature of a considerable number of the canonical
psalms on which this collection is based, but may also reflect the
social and historical situation of the circles in which these hymns
were promulgated. They describe themselves as more devout than
many of their contemporaries (8.23, 34; 10.6; 12.4; 14.3; 15.7), for
example, and emphasize their fear of God (3.12; 6.5; 13.12; cf. 3.3),
humility (3.8; 5.12), faithfulness to the law (14.2–3) and willingness
to undertake voluntary acts of piety such as fasting (3.8). They regard
God as being particularly concerned for the poor and needy (e.g.
5.2, 11; 15.1; 16.13–14), a view which is rooted in their study of the
Scriptures, but which may also signify that they considered themselves
to be poor or marginalized. This self-understanding may partly
explain their criticism of the excessive wealth of their opponents and
of perceived social injustices (e.g. 1.4; 5.16).

The last two of these psalms are of particular significance for the
evidence they provide about the eschatological expectation current
in at least some Jewish circles in this period. *Psalms of Solomon* 17
offers an unusually detailed insight into the author's hopes that God
will intervene decisively in the current situation by sending a Messiah,
a new Davidic king, who will expel the gentile rulers and then reign
over the people of Israel in wisdom and righteousness (17.23–32).
This figure will receive divine strength to drive out the foreign
invaders (17.22), make other nations serve him (17.30) and bring
back the Jews living in the Diaspora (17.31). Sinless himself (17.36),

he will be able to lead the people to holiness (17.26, 30, 32, 41) in recognition that their ultimate king is God (17.1, 46).

Commentators often point to the military prowess associated with this future saviour, who will 'purge Jerusalem from gentiles' (17.22), 'smash the arrogance of sinners like a potter's jar . . . with an iron rod' (17.23) and tolerate no unrighteousness (17.27). This is only one aspect of the overall picture, however, since the text also indicates that the Messiah will be compassionate to the gentile nations who accept him (17.34) and that he will not need to rely on his armies, since God is his real strength:

> He will not rely on horse and rider and bow,
> Nor will he collect gold and silver for war.
> Nor will he build up hope in a multitude for a day of war.
> The Lord himself is his king,
> The hope of one who has a strong hope in God.
>
> (17.33–4)

It is also important to recognize that, in much of this section, the psalmist is simply drawing on scriptural imagery and language, echoing especially Isaiah 11.1–5, which looks forward to the coming of a righteous ruler, who fears God, judges with wisdom and impartiality, and 'shall smite the earth with the rod of his mouth, and with the breath of his lips he shall slay the wicked' (Isa. 11.4; cf. Ps. 2.9).

Scriptural sources such as Psalm 72 and the account of Solomon's reign in 1 Kings 2—11 may have provided the model for this description of the ideal king, since Solomon is described there as David's son and designated heir, renowned for his wisdom and just judgements, who built a temple in Jerusalem, extended Israel's boundaries and received tribute from the rulers of other nations. The author's messianic expectations probably reflect a belief in the continuing validity of the promise of everlasting Davidic kingship (e.g. 2 Sam. 7.8–16; Ps. 89.19–37), since the kings of the legitimate Davidic line are explicitly contrasted at the beginning of *Psalms of Solomon* 17 with the current rulers of Israel who are said to have arrogantly usurped the throne (17.4–6). These hopes are also very likely to have been shaped in response to a historical and political situation in which the country's leadership was perceived as weak, violent or corrupt, and so not able to deliver freedom and justice for Israel.

The experiences of life in the first century BCE either under Hasmonaean rule and/or under the Romans and Herod may have prompted severe dissatisfaction with the status quo and a longing for transformative divine intervention. Similar expectation of an ideal Davidic king is, for example, attested in several of the Dead Sea Scrolls dating from this period.[8]

These developing Jewish beliefs about the anointed one (*messiah* in Hebrew, *christos* in Greek) are of particular interest to New Testament scholars because they form the backdrop to early Christian claims about Jesus. The phrase 'and their king shall be the Lord Messiah [or Messiah Lord]' (17.32; cf. 18.7 and the heading for *Pss. Sol.* 18), for example, may be an early precedent for the use in the New Testament of the title 'Christ the Lord' or 'Lord Jesus Christ' (as found frequently in Paul's letters; see also Luke 2.11).[9] The extensive description of the future reign of the Messiah in *Psalms of Solomon* 17 is, then, a particularly interesting feature of the theology of this work, but its presence as a theme within the collection should not be overemphasized, since he is referred to only very briefly in one other hymn (18.5–8).

The *Sibylline Oracles*

Introduction to the *Sibylline Oracles*

This work consists of a relatively large collection of Jewish and early Christian oracles written in Greek and attributed to a female prophet or sibyl. The oldest extant manuscripts date from the late mediaeval period, but the contents cover an earlier and very long time-span, between the second century BCE and the seventh century CE. Sibylline prophecy itself is an even older phenomenon, reaching back to a tradition which probably arose in Greece, but which was popular with all classes in society throughout the ancient world, especially in Italy and Asia Minor. One of the most famous pagan prophetesses, the Erythrean Sibyl, figures in Virgil's *Aeneid* (6.1–55), for example,

---

[8] For further detail, see J. J. Collins, *The Scepter and the Star: Messianism in the Light of the Dead Sea Scrolls.* 2nd edn. 2010, Grand Rapids, Michigan; Eerdmans.

[9] Several commentators assume that the original Hebrew underlying this phrase was the more common 'Messiah *of* the Lord', but even if this is the case, it is still significant that a Greek translator employed the title 'Messiah Lord' (*christos kurios*).

and an official written anthology of sibylline oracles was kept in the temple of Jupiter Capitolinus in Rome for several centuries and consulted for insight, only by permission of the Senate, in times of military, political or social crisis.

The origin of the term 'sibyl' is uncertain, but it may have been the proper name of an early prophetess. The sibyls were all women, usually having the prestige of old age, who were thought to be inspired to utter ecstatic revelations. Their words tended to be messages of doom rather than good news, with many oracles describing past or future wars and natural catastrophes, and others commenting negatively on human behaviour. Their ongoing relevance was secured by the ease with which the often vague or opaque sayings could be reworked or added to in different circumstances. Only isolated fragments of the pagan oracles have survived, but it seems that they were generally quite short, just a line or two in length. Jews, especially those living in Egypt, adopted the sibylline genre in order to provide a sense of authority and antiquity for their history and religion. They made important adaptations to the form, however, placing more emphasis on ethical teaching and eschatological expectation, and weaving in scriptural allusions. Sibylline oracles remained popular among early Christians, who shaped them to include prophecies about Christ, thereby implying that even pagans foretold his coming. Several church fathers quoted them extensively, and five pagan sibyls are depicted alongside the Old Testament prophets in Michelangelo's decoration of the Sistine Chapel. The Judaeo-Christian appropriation of the genre is illustrated by the claim that one of the sibyls was a daughter-in-law of Noah (Prologue, lines 33–5; 1.287–91; 3.823–8).

The *Sibylline Oracles* consists of 12 short books, numbered 1 to 8 and then 11 to 14; numbers 9 and 10 are generally omitted from the standard collection because they simply repeat material from earlier sections. Books 3, 4 and 5 will be considered in detail here, since these are the only parts of the anthology which are definitely Jewish works dating from the Second Temple period. The rest of the compilation includes a Christian Prologue written no earlier than the sixth century CE, which outlines the origins of the sibylline literature and explains that the oracles were regarded as early testimony to Jesus (lines 15–23). Books 1 to 2 are usually dated to the second century CE and treated as a unit. In their current form they are Christian (see especially 1.324–400), although in the view of many scholars they do contain material which is originally Jewish. They recount the history of humanity from creation to the present time, dividing it into ten generations (see also e.g. 3.156–61), a pattern which is familiar from pagan sibylline literature and is also used in apocalyptic writing (e.g. the Apocalypse of Weeks in *1 En.* 93.3–14; 91.12–17). Considerable attention is given to the flood narrative and the righteousness of Noah. Book 2 describes the many natural disasters and wars which will characterize the tenth generation of humanity (2.6–26), and looks forward to eschatological signs and a final judgement (2.154–359). Books 6, 7 and 8 are Christian compositions dating from the second or third century CE, which include hymns to Christ (6.1–28; 8.217–358), eschatological sections and warnings of doom directed against various nations. Some originally Jewish oracles may have been preserved in the first half of Book 8, which is characterized by strong criticism of Rome's cruel domination of other countries and socially unjust rule (8.36–159).

Books 11 to 14 form a group, as together they offer a review of history from the time of the flood to the Arab conquest of Egypt in the seventh century CE. This material was almost certainly composed at different times in the early centuries CE, and sometimes draws on previous sibylline literature, especially Book 3, illustrating the way in which this fluid tradition was continually being adapted for new contexts. Commentators such as John Collins attribute these four books to Egyptian Jewish circles, although this is not certain, and in the case of Book 13 there are no clear indications of either Christian or Jewish authorship. Book 11 interweaves stories from Graeco-Roman literature, such as the birth of Romulus and Remus (11.109–17) and the Trojan War (11.122–63; see also a short passage in praise of the wisdom of Virgil, 11.164–71), with allusions to the Scriptures (e.g. the flood and the Tower of Babel, 11.6–14) and thinly veiled references to historical figures like Alexander (11.195–223) and Cleopatra (11.246–60). Its core may date from before the Christian era. Book 12 comments on the Roman emperors from Augustus to Alexander Severus, denouncing unpopular rulers such as Caligula (12.48–67) and Nero (12.78–94), but giving a generally favourable picture of most of the others. Book 13 continues with accounts of revolts against Roman rule in the mid-third century BCE, but the extant text of Book 14 is very corrupt, making it difficult to interpret. The *Sibylline Oracles* as a whole is of great interest for the light it sheds on both Jewish and Christian thought in the early centuries BCE and CE, and for the way it combines pagan, Jewish and Christian elements.

Key features of the *Sibylline Oracles* Books 3–5

The *Sibylline Oracles* were written in verse, in the hexameter metre commonly used in ancient Graeco-Roman poetry. Not only did their Jewish authors take over this classical poetic form and an originally pagan genre, but they readily drew on Greek literature more widely, including, for instance, references to the myths about the Titans (3.110–58) and to the Trojan War (3.401–33; cf. 11.109–71). These works demonstrate a spirit similar to the *Exagoge*, then, of willingness to engage with Hellenistic culture and a desire to find common ground between Jews and gentiles.

Unsurprisingly, some similarities can be seen between the *Sibylline Oracles* and the prophetic books of the Old Testament, since the sibyls and the Israelite prophets alike claimed to be inspired to proclaim the words of God to the people of their time. Thus references to ecstatic utterances and an irresistible compulsion to speak occur throughout this literature, as in the opening lines of Book 3:

> But why does my heart shake again? And why is my spirit
> lashed by a whip, compelled from within to proclaim
> an oracle to all? But I will utter everything again,
> as much as God bids me to say to men.
>
> (3.4–7; cf. 2.1–5; 3.162–5, 295–300,
> 489–92; 4.18–24; 5.52)[10]

The way in which the *Sibylline Oracles* took shape also parallels in some respects the formation of the scriptural prophetic literature, with a core of early sayings receiving expansion over time as older material was updated for new circumstances.[11]

---

[10] All translations of the texts are taken from J. J. Collins, 'The Sibylline Oracles'. In *The Old Testament Pseudepigrapha Vol. 1*. Ed. J. H. Charlesworth. 1983, New York: Doubleday, pp. 317–472.

[11] For this view, see esp. E. S. Gruen, *Heritage and Hellenism: The Reinvention of Jewish Tradition*. 1998, Berkeley: University of California Press.

One of the most characteristic features of the sibylline genre is the frequent announcement of impending judgement and disaster for specific people or cities (e.g. 3.205–10, 300–80, 493–544; 5.54–135, 160–213, 287–359, 434–46), exemplified by this threat to Babylon:

> Woe to you, Babylon, of golden throne and golden sandal.
> For many years you were the sole kingdom ruling over the world.
> You who were formerly great and universal, you will no longer lie
> on golden mountains and streams of the Euphrates.
> You will be spread out flat by the turmoil of an earthquake ...
> (5.434–8)

These 'woe-passages' can be compared to the oracles against the nations recorded in several of the prophetic books (see e.g. Isa. 13—23; Jer. 46—51; Ezek. 25—31; Amos 1—2). There are also many connections of form and theme between this literature and apocalypses (see below, Chapter 6), such as the view that history is divided into predetermined periods and the frequent descriptions of the signs of the end and future judgement. Other typical elements of the apocalyptic genre are lacking in the *Sibylline Oracles*, however, such as visions or the presence of interpreting angels. This is a further reminder of the frequent overlap and permeability of the literary genres employed within the corpus of early Jewish writings.

Important themes in the *Sibylline Oracles* Books 3–5

These three books are made up of material dating from a range of time periods and geographical regions, so they naturally contain different emphases and even take contrary positions on some themes. However, since they are also part of a shared sibylline tradition, some common motifs and relationships between them can be discerned and are highlighted here. Both the theological ideas and the historical information contained in the sibylline literature are of great value for an understanding of Second Temple Judaism.

Book 3

Book 3 is the longest and the oldest book in the present collection of *Sibylline Oracles*. Probably composed by Jews in Egypt,[12] it incorporates

---

[12] The main dissenter from this view among modern commentators is Rieuwerd Buitenwerf, who argues that its provenance is Asia Minor in the mid-first century BCE; see his *Book III of the Sibylline Oracles and Its Social Setting*. 2003, Leiden: Brill.

sayings from different centuries, including some earlier pagan sibylline sources. Lines 97–349 and 489–829 are generally considered
to form the book's original core, and are dated to the mid-second
century BCE. Another section, largely made up of oracles against various nations (3.350–488), was added in the late first century BCE.
The introduction (3.1–96) reviews God's creation of the world and
the origins of humanity, and may formerly have been part of a
separate book. Sections of Book 3 can be dated quite precisely by
their references to known historical figures and events. In the later
sections (3.350–488), for instance, severe criticism is levelled against
the dominant world powers of the time, Rome and Asia Minor (e.g.
3.350–400; cf. 3.46–62); anti-Roman sentiment in particular is a
recurring theme also in later sibylline literature (see Books 4, 5, 8).
In both Jewish and gentile contexts, then, sibylline oracles could
take on a political dimension, as they encourage an expectation of
a definite reversal of fortune for the current ruling elites after history
has run its appointed course (see e.g. 3.156–61).

One such passage in Book 3 has generated particular interest
among commentators. It foretells the arrival of 'a king from the sun'
who will act 'in obedience to the noble teachings of the great God'
to end all wars and rule over the entire earth (3.652–6). His reign
appears to mark the start of the eschaton, the age of final judgement
and blessings for the righteous (3.657–808). This saying is widely
interpreted as an allusion to a ruler belonging to the native Egyptian
Ptolemaic dynasty, not least because of the long association of the
pharaohs with the sun. Partly on the basis of other references in
the text to a seventh king of Egypt (3.193, 318, 608), this figure is
often identified specifically with Ptolemy VI Philometor who reigned
over Egypt from 163 to 145 BCE, and is thought to have enjoyed
good relationships with the Jewish community there, providing the
land for Onias to build the temple in Heliopolis, for example. It
would indeed be a significant theological development for a Jewish
author to hail a gentile ruler as a divinely sent saviour, although it
would not be a statement without scriptural precedent, given the
designation of the Persian ruler Cyrus as 'God's anointed' in Isaiah
45.1 (cf. *Sib. Or.* 3.286). The oracle is quite ambiguous, however,
so it is not accepted by all commentators as evidence of a definite
expectation by some Diaspora Jews of an Egyptian saviour king.

As with many of the Jewish writings of this period, a stress on monotheism lies at the heart of the theological and ethical outlook of the editors of *Sibylline Oracles* Book 3. Thus the text condemns idolatry unreservedly, ridiculing the worship of objects made by human hands in terms which allude to the Scriptures (e.g. 3.29–35, 277–9, 547–8, 586–90, 605–7; cf. e.g. Pss. 115.4–8; 135.15–17; Isa. 40.18–20; 44.9–20; Jer. 10.3–9; Dan. 5.23). However, the one God whom the Jews worship is often described in language familiar from Greek philosophy. God is, for example, frequently called 'the immortal one' (e.g. 3.10, 55, 283, 600, 617, 631, 694, 708, 717, 743, 757, 766), and, although the Prologue probably does not share the same provenance as the rest of the book, its philosophical introduction to God is a striking example of the way Jewish sibylline literature interacts with Hellenistic thought:

> There is one God, sole ruler, ineffable, who lives in the sky,
> Self-begotten, invisible, who himself sees all things . . .
>
> (3.11–12)

Similarly, much of the moral teaching put forward in the text would have been acceptable to both Jews and gentiles, for example:

> For all good order and righteous dealing will come
> upon men from starry heaven and with it
> temperate concord, best of all things for men
> and love, faithfulness and friendship even from strangers.
> Bad government, blame, envy, anger, folly,
> poverty will flee from men, and constraint will flee,
> and murder, accursed strife, and grievous quarrels,
> night robberies, and every evil in those days.   (3.373–80)

Such passages imply that there is some shared sense among Jews and their fellow-citizens of what kind of behaviour is harmful to society and what virtues human beings should aspire to.

Definite aspects of Stoic thought are also present in the text, including the idea that 'the heavenly one gave the earth in common to all' (3.261). More specifically Jewish attitudes are reflected elsewhere, however, and their engagement with Graeco-Roman culture does not dilute the authors' commitment to Torah and tradition. This is evident in the dismissal of practices such as astrology and fortune-telling as futile (3.221–34), for instance, and in the fact that the sins of homosexuality (3.185–6, 596–600, 764), sexual immorality (3.43–5, 595, 764) and infanticide (3.765) are singled out for censure and associated with gentiles in particular.

Other oracles demonstrate the same kind of concern for social justice as is found throughout the Scriptures (e.g. 3.40–1, 189, 630, 783), so that, for example, a eulogy on the superior righteousness of the Jews over other peoples emphasizes their commitment to fair dealing and generosity to the poor, and cites love for money as the cause of many evils (3.239–47). Obedience to the Mosaic laws as divinely given is urged (3.256–9; cf. 3.246, 284, 580, 719, 768), and the traditional explanation that it was the failure of the people of Israel in past generations to keep the commandments which led to their exile is echoed here (3.266–82), as is the belief that those who follow them now will be rewarded, while those who do not will face punishment and destruction:

> And if anyone should disobey
> he would pay the penalty by law, whether at human hands
> or escaping men he would be utterly destroyed in all justice . . .
> For these alone the fertile soil yields fruit
> From one- to a hundredfold, and the measures of God are
>   produced.   (3.258–60, 263–4)

Another noticeable theme in the sibylline literature is the prominence of the Temple. Book 3 exemplifies the view that it is central to Jewish life and religion: its beauty and wealth is praised (e.g. 3.575–9, 657–8), and nations like Babylon are condemned for having attacked it (e.g. 3.266, 274–95, 302, 665). The Temple is particularly emphasized in descriptions of the eschatological age. In a strong echo of scriptural language, it is associated with peace (e.g. 3.702–3, 727–31; cf. Isa. 2.4; Ezek. 39.9–10; Mic. 4.3–4), and the hope is expressed that in the future gentiles will stream to it to worship the one true God (e.g. 3.715–27; cf. Isa. 2.2–3; Mic. 4.2).

These oracles seem to reflect a universalist theological stance, and a belief in the ultimate conversion to Judaism of at least some gentiles, but, interestingly, scholars are divided in their opinions about the attitude of the book as a whole to Hellenistic culture. A minority focus on the harsh critique offered throughout of idolatry and the immorality of gentile nations, and on the commitment to the Jerusalem

Temple and to the national and religious superiority of the Jews. John Barclay, for instance, sees these elements as indicating a high level of alienation from Egyptian society on the part of this Jewish community, whose members have learned to their cost that 'everyone will be offended at your customs' (3.272).[13] The majority of commentators, however, including John Collins and George Nickelsburg,[14] argue that, in both form and content, the book shows a remarkable openness to gentiles and to contemporary culture, as well as a favourable attitude to the ruling Ptolemaic house of Egypt, exemplified by the expectation of a future 'king from the sun'.

Book 4

Sibylline Oracles Book 4 takes up some of these same themes, notably the criticism of idolatry (4.5–7, 27–30), an expectation of a coming age of judgement for the wicked and salvation for the righteous (4.40–6, 171–90), and hostility towards the ruling powers, especially Macedonia (4.76–101) and Rome (4.102–51). It is difficult to date this book precisely, since it appears to be a compilation of material from various times and sources. At its core is probably a pagan sibylline oracle which takes a political and anti-Macedonian stance (4.49–101) and which has been updated and expanded by Jewish editors in different periods. References to identifiable historical events in the first century CE, such as the fall of Jerusalem (4.115–16, 125–7) and the eruption of Vesuvius (4.130–1), can be used to help date these later additions. The division of history into generations and kingdoms which is characteristic of both sibylline and apocalyptic literature is in evidence here (see especially 4.49–114).

There is no direct reference to the Mosaic law, and the ethical injunctions are rather more general than those found in Book 3, but similar moral values are highlighted: dishonest gain is described as an abominable act on a level with murder, for instance, and adultery

---

[13] J. M. G. Barclay, *Jews in the Mediterranean Diaspora from Alexander to Trajan (323 BCE–117 CE)*. 1996, Berkeley: University of California Press.

[14] See e.g. J. J. Collins, *Between Athens and Jerusalem: Jewish Identity in the Hellenistic Diaspora*. 2nd edn. 2000, Grand Rapids, Michigan: Eerdmans, pp. 83–166; and G. W. E. Nickelsburg, *Jewish Literature between the Bible and the Mishnah*. 2nd edn. 2005, Minneapolis: Fortress Press, pp. 193–6.

and homosexuality are also condemned (4.31–4). One noticeable difference from other sibylline texts is that Book 4 does not celebrate the importance of the Temple. On the contrary, it is specifically stated here that God does not have a house on earth (4.8–11) and that those who love God 'reject all temples . . . altars, too, useless foundations of dumb stones' (4.27–8). These sayings could well be directed against pagan worship rather than the Jerusalem Temple, but this attitude may also reflect the historical context in which they were produced, perhaps in the aftermath of the destruction of the city by the Romans, when alternative means of establishing Jewish identity were required.

There is a final exhortation to repentance which is also interesting theologically, since it calls on its hearers to 'wash your whole bodies in perennial rivers . . . and ask forgiveness for your previous deeds' (4.165). This link between water and conversion of life seems to echo the message attributed to John the Baptist in the New Testament, prompting some commentators to associate Book 4 with Diaspora Jewish baptist circles, although there is little extant evidence for the activity of such groups.

Book 5

Book 5 is generally dated to the late first or early second century CE, as it makes specific references to Roman emperors of this period, such as Nero (e.g. 5.28–34) and Hadrian (5.46–50), and to events such as the destruction of the Temple in 70 CE (5.398–413). There is some minor Christian redaction, in a reference to Jesus' crucifixion (5.256–9), but the Jewish origin of Book 5 is generally accepted by commentators. It opens with a characteristically sibylline review of history from the time of Alexander the Great to the present (5.1–51), and the oracles which follow consist largely of warnings of doom against various nations and descriptions of the coming eschatological age. Its provenance is likely to have been Egypt (see e.g. 5.2–3, 17–18, 53, 484–511), but it does not share the positive view of that country expressed in parts of Book 3, and instead details Egypt's sins and foretells its impending destruction alongside that of other nations (5.52–98, 179–99). This attitude may reflect the fact that relationships between Jews and gentiles in Egypt and various other regions of the Roman Empire were strained at this time, as evidenced by the Jewish revolts in Egypt, Cyprus and Mesopotamia in 115–17 CE.

The greatest hostility is reserved for Rome, however, which is accused in bitter terms of all kinds of immorality, especially arrogance, and castigated for destroying Jerusalem and its Temple (see especially 5.159–78, 386–99). The complete annihilation of the empire is therefore predicted (5.168–78; cf. Isa. 47.1–15). Such views are expressed elsewhere in sibylline literature, as already noted, and it is interesting also to compare this passage to parts of the New Testament which are approximately contemporary with *Sibylline Oracles* Book 5, such as the warning of the fall of Babylon or Rome in chapter 18 of the book of Revelation, especially as both writings also hope for the restoration of a glorious Jerusalem (5.249–55, 420–7; cf. Rev. 21).

These descriptions of future judgement and salvation are a particularly significant feature of Book 5. As in Book 3, but in contrast to Book 4, the Temple has a place in the future expectation of this text (5.501–11; cf. 5.398–413, 433) and it also looks to the arrival of a saviour, but not the gentile ruler of Book 3. Rather, these oracles hope for the coming from heaven (5.256–9, 414–25) of a Jewish king (5.108–9) called the 'star' (5.155–61; cf. Num. 24.7; *T. Jud.* 24.1; CD 7.18–21) to completely transform the situation for the faithful. This picture has affinities with the tradition of a heavenly Messiah represented by, for example, Daniel chapters 7 and 12, or the Qumran *War Scroll* (1QM). It might indicate that the community behind this text felt that their situation was so hopeless that only a direct supernatural intervention could bring about the required change in fortune, but a restoration of this earth is still expected (5.249–55, 420–7).

In several oracles, the saviour is said to be preceded by an eschatological adversary. This figure is often identified with a Nero *redivivus* (see e.g. 5.361–85), but Jan Willem van Henten has argued that the *Sibylline Oracles* do not illustrate a belief that the actual Emperor Nero would one day return to earth, but instead a tendency for negative stereotypes of Nero and other tyrants to be recycled and applied to later emperors and future rulers (see e.g. 5.28–50, 93–110, 214–28; cf. 8.50–159). On this reading of the text, its message is that another ruler as evil and destructive as Nero was can be expected as part of the enacting of divine judgement on the world.[15]

Other examples of poetic, hymnic and dramatic texts

A rich tradition of composing prayers and hymns flourished in Second Temple Judaism. Previous chapters of this volume have demonstrated, for instance, how new prayers were added when the Scriptures were retold or expanded, and this feature also characterizes the deutero-canonical literature, which contains examples such as the Prayer of Azariah and the Song of the Three Young Men in the Greek Additions to the book of Daniel. An important collection of hymns from this period has also been discovered at Qumran (1QH). Composed in Hebrew in the first or second century BCE, this work is known as the *Thanksgiving Hymns* (Hebrew *Hodayot*) because of the frequent occurrence in it of the refrain 'I thank you, Lord'. It seems to have included at least 30 psalms, although it is difficult to determine the exact number, because the seven copies found are all fragmentary. Like the *Psalms of Solomon*, these prayers are modelled on the canonical psalms, especially the individual thanksgiving songs, and were presumably used within community worship. They contain literally hundreds of scriptural allusions, drawing particularly heavily on the Psalms, Isaiah and Deuteronomy. The first person singular is widely used throughout, although this may represent the collective consciousness of the Qumran sect as much as the outpouring of any one individual.

There are some similarities of thought and outlook between the *Hodayot* and the *Psalms of Solomon*. Both collections, for example, reflect the view that the world is divided into two groups, the righteous or poor, who keep God's commandments and are blessed and saved by God, and their adversaries who are sinners and far from God. The Qumran psalmists also often thank God for delivering them from the trials and sufferings inflicted upon them by their enemies, and look forward to future divine intervention and judgement. Some further interesting aspects of the theology of the Qumran

---

[15] See J. W. van Henten, 'Nero *Redivivus* Demolished: The Coherence of the Nero Traditions in the *Sibylline Oracles*'. *JSP* 21 (2000), pp. 3–17.

community are in evidence, such as the authors' belief that they already shared fellowship with the angels (e.g. 1QH 11.23).

The significance of the non-narrative literature

This chapter has highlighted the very creative use of non-narrative forms of writing by Jews living both in Palestine and in the Diaspora. The *Exagoge* and the *Sibylline Oracles* are particularly interesting for their confident engagement with Hellenistic culture and education. These authors and editors adopted Graeco-Roman literary genres, were influenced by gentile religious language and forms, and accepted that Hellenistic myths and literature could be appreciated and referred to alongside Scripture. It is not, therefore, surprising that the *Sibylline Oracles* echoes one strand of the Scriptures in expressing its hope for the ultimate salvation of gentiles (e.g. 3.715–27), a view which was to prove so important later for the growth of Christianity. These early attempts to employ contemporary literary forms to educate people about Jewish history and beliefs in an engaging way can even be seen as a forerunner of more modern attempts to present Bible stories through the medium of film or rap songs, for example. In addition, the *Exagoge* is a significant text for classical scholars, because, as the most extensive surviving example of a Greek tragedy, it can illuminate the historical development of that genre: it suggests, for example, that earlier views about an ideal drama being confined to one geographical location and a period of no more than 24 hours (see e.g. Aristotle, *Poetics* 1449b) may have been changing by the time it was composed.

The writings considered in this chapter are also significant for the evidence they provide about the attitudes of Jews in different contexts to the ruling powers and political events of their time. Neither the *Sibylline Oracles* nor the *Psalms of Solomon* holds back from scathing criticism of political and religious elites, whether Jewish or gentile, or of perceived social ills, even warning of the utter destruction of the imperial capital city Rome (5.162–78). These texts may well have been considered subversive in their time, and they serve as a reminder of the long history behind that strand of Judaism and later Christianity which has engaged in social critique, rooted in biblical teaching on justice. Sometimes they provide important confirmation of information given in other sources, such as the references in *Psalms of Solomon* 8 to the warm welcome initially offered to the Roman general Pompey by some of the Jewish religious leaders, which support the account in Josephus' *Antiquities* (*Ant.* 14.3).

Since all three of these texts allude to Scripture in different ways, drawing heavily on its themes and language, they demonstrate the historical evolution of exegetical traditions, such as those reflected in the *Exagoge* relating to Moses' early education, or his striking the water with his staff. They also attest to important theological developments, not least the reflections on disasters as a punishment for sin found in both the *Psalms of Solomon* and the *Sibylline Oracles*. It is interesting, for instance, to find in the *Psalms of Solomon* evidence of a devout Jewish community whose members were not totally satisfied with the traditional explanations for suffering, so introduced a distinction between God's punishment of the wicked and a cleansing fatherly discipline for the righteous. This problem of innocent suffering has continued to occupy Jewish theologians even into the current era, in the light of horrifying catastrophes such as the Holocaust, which cannot be justified as a divine response to human sin.

All this provides further evidence of the diversity which characterized the theology and worship of Jews throughout the Second Temple period. It has proved difficult, for instance, to attribute any of these writings to a particular known group such as the Pharisees or Essenes, and the *Exagoge* has thrown up the intriguing possibility of an early mystical strain within Diaspora Judaism, centred on speculation about Moses. The views expressed by these authors here can often illuminate the background of thought to New Testament ideas, as in the case of the references to repentance accompanied by baptism and the hope for a restored and glorious Jerusalem in the *Sibylline Oracles* (4.162–70; 5.420–7). Particularly significant in this regard is the variety of messianic expectation reflected in these texts, since *Psalms of Solomon* 17 provides the most detailed extant description of a Davidic Messiah, while passages in the *Sibylline Oracles* look forward variously to either a heavenly saviour figure (e.g. 5.414) or a gentile king who will usher in the final age (3.652–6).

Further reading

Atkinson, K., *An Intertextual Study of the Psalms of Solomon.* 2000, Lewiston, New York: Edwin Mellen Press

Barclay, J. M. G., *Jews in the Mediterranean Diaspora from Alexander to Trajan (323 BCE–117 CE).* 1996, Berkeley: University of California Press

Collins, J. J., *The Scepter and the Star: Messianism in the Light of the Dead Sea Scrolls.* 2nd edn. 2010, Grand Rapids, Michigan; Eerdmans

Collins, J. J., *The Sibylline Oracles of Egyptian Judaism.* 1974, Missoula: Society of Biblical Literature

Jacobson, H., *The Exagoge of Ezekiel.* 1983, Cambridge: Cambridge University Press

Nickelsburg, G. W. E., *Jewish Literature between the Bible and the Mishnah.* 2nd edn. 2005, Minneapolis: Fortress Press

Robertson, R. G., 'Ezekiel the Tragedian'. In *The Old Testament Pseudepigrapha Vol. 2.* Ed. J. H. Charlesworth. 1985, New York: Doubleday, pp. 803–19

5

Testaments

Introducing the testament genre

The label 'testament' is attached to those early Jewish and Christian writings which present a deathbed speech of a patriarch or other important scriptural figure, in which he offers moral instruction and future predictions to his gathered descendants. This framework seems to be inspired by biblical passages like Genesis 49, in which Jacob is seen calling his sons together for a final blessing (see also the farewell speech of Moses in Deut. 34). Such texts perhaps indicate the importance attached in ancient cultures to the authority of the ancestors and to the proper transmission of inheritance and traditions.[1]

The testament form is, however, rather difficult to define, and some scholars even question whether such a genre really exists, since there are relatively few examples of it, all of which differ from one another in several respects and also contain elements of other types of writing, especially apocalyptic. The extant examples of testamentary literature do, however, generally share a similar narrative outline, opening with a scene in which the protagonist, on the point of dying, gathers his family around his bed to hear his last words, and concluding with an account of his death and burial. They vary considerably in terms of content, but often include a blend of ethical teaching and eschatological expectation. The genre is attested in early Christianity as well as Second Temple Judaism, and some New Testament commentators have taken an interest in it, as it may provide an illuminating context for passages like the farewell

---

[1] It has also been suggested that the structure is a development of the Old Testament covenant formula (e.g. Exod. 6.2–8; 19.4–6; 20.1–17; Lev. 26.1–46; Deut. 4.1–40; 11.1–32), in which the rehearsal of the mighty deeds of God or the sovereign has been replaced by a biographical account of the patriarch's life, but the exhortation to obedience in order to obtain future reward is retained. However, the narrative form of the testamentary literature and its lack of specific focus on the covenant laws mean that it does not really fit this pattern. See K. Baltzer, *The Covenant Formulary in Old Testament, Jewish and Early Christian Writings.* 1971, Oxford: Blackwell.

discourses in the Fourth Gospel (John 13—17) or Paul's speech at Miletus (Acts 20.17–37). All the extant writings from the Second Temple period which now bear the title 'testament' will be considered in this chapter, although a strong case could be made for including the *Testament of Moses* instead under the heading of apocalyptic.

The *Testaments of the Twelve Patriarchs*

Introduction to the *Testaments of the Twelve Patriarchs*

This is another example of a work which was traditionally ascribed to Jewish authorship, but which is now widely regarded as a product of early Christianity (see also the debate about *The Life of Adam and Eve* and the *Ascension of Isaiah* in Chapter 3, above). In its current form, there is no doubting that the *Testaments of the Twelve Patriarchs* is a Christian composition: it was preserved and transmitted only by Christians, and it contains several clear references to Jesus, commenting, for example, on his coming to earth as a man (*T. Sim.* 6.5) and his crucifixion (*T. Levi* 4.4). Such texts of disputed provenance are, however, often included in volumes dealing with the literature of Second Temple Judaism when they seem to contain a substantial amount of originally Jewish material, as is the case with the *Testaments of the Twelve Patriarchs*, which closely resembles some extant Jewish writings, especially the *Aramaic Levi Document* found both at Qumran and among the mediaeval manuscripts of the Cairo Genizah.

The extent to which the present Christian work depends on pre-existing sources and incorporates older traditions remains a matter of scholarly debate. All that can be stated with certainty is that it was written in Greek, probably in the early second century CE, since it is quoted by the church father Origen in about 250 CE (Origen, *Homilies on Joshua* 15.6). It therefore provides significant evidence for the theological views and ethical values current among Christians at that time. It survives in a small number of Greek manuscripts, the oldest of which dates from the tenth century CE, and also in Armenian, Slavonic, Serbian and Latin versions.

The text presents the fictional deathbed speeches of each of the sons of Jacob, in age order, beginning with Reuben the firstborn through to Benjamin the youngest. It is, therefore, a collection of 12 individual 'testaments', some of which may have circulated separately before being brought together, although a certain unity of form and theme has been imposed on them here. Each ancestor is pictured reflecting aloud on key events in his life, drawing both on material found in the biblical book of Genesis and on later exegetical traditions, and using these experiences as the basis for his final words of advice, encouragement or warning for his descendants.

Key features of the *Testaments of the Twelve Patriarchs*

This work is often taken as the model of the testament genre, as each section includes a deathbed speech by a patriarch, autobiographical information, ethical exhortation, future predictions and an account of his burial. The testaments are of differing lengths, with those attributed to Levi and Judah being the most extensive. This is probably a reflection of the prominence of these two figures in Jewish thought, and the consequent availability of a wealth of pre-existing traditions relating to them.

There is naturally considerable allusion throughout the *Testaments of the Twelve Patriarchs* to the Genesis narratives, but the story of Joseph takes on a particular importance, so that the behaviour towards him of each of his brothers becomes a decisive factor in the evaluation of their characters. There are also echoes of the language, themes and forms typical of the biblical wisdom literature, especially in the exhortatory sections. The opening of the *Testament of Joseph* (1.1—2.7) is structured like an individual thanksgiving psalm, for instance, and the description of the way of life of the righteous or genuine man in the *Testament of Issachar* (4.1–6) resembles several passages in Proverbs and Psalms (cf. *T. Sim.* 6.2–4; *T. Levi* 13.1–9; *T. Naph.* 8.7–8). The Enochic writings also appear to have been valued by the circles behind these testaments, since the 'Books of Enoch the Righteous' are frequently appealed to as a source of authority or further information (see e.g. *T. Sim.* 5.4; *T. Levi* 10.5; 14.1; *T. Jud.* 18.1; *T. Dan* 5.6; *T. Naph.* 4.1; *T. Benj.* 9.1; cf. *T. Reu.* 5.6). Interestingly, it is often impossible to connect these references to anything in the extant Enochic literature. This may indicate that a wider tradition associated with Enoch once existed but has now been lost, so is a useful reminder of the partial nature of the evidence for the theology and practice of Second Temple Judaism, a fact highlighted also by the discovery of the Qumran Scrolls which lay hidden for so many centuries.

Important themes in the *Testaments of the Twelve Patriarchs*

The most prominent theme in the *Testaments of the Twelve Patriarchs* is undoubtedly its ethical teaching. The lives of the patriarchs are put forward as exemplars of particular virtues or vices, which their children are then exhorted to either imitate or avoid. The *Testament of Reuben*, for instance, expands on the brief notice in Genesis of Reuben's illicit sexual relationship with his father's concubine Bilhah (Gen. 35.22), and uses this incident as a warning against the dangers of alcohol, youthful foolishness and feminine wiles.

The ethical values advocated throughout all the testaments can be summed up in the ideal of love of both God and one's neighbour (e.g. *T. Reu.* 6.8–9; *T. Iss.* 5.1–2; 7.6–7; *T. Dan* 5.2–3; *T. Gad* 4.1–2; *T. Jos.* 11.1; *T. Benj.* 3.3–4; 10.2–3). In this presentation of patriarchal instruction, it is virtually indistinguishable from the general moral norms of Graeco-Roman society. The qualities promoted include, for instance, temperance and purity (*T. Jud.*), simplicity of life (*T. Iss.*), generosity to the poor (*T. Zeb.*), single-mindedness (*T. Ash.*), and chastity, endurance and mercy (*T. Jos.*), while behaviour such as lack of self-control (*T. Jud.*), envy (*T. Sim.*), greed (*T. Jud.*), falsehood (*T. Dan*) and anger (*T. Gad*) is condemned. There is no teaching related to specifically Jewish or Christian practices, such as sabbath, circumcision, diet or worship, although idolatry and intermarriage are occasionally denounced. Many commentators, therefore, suggest that the text circulated in communities characterized by an open and universalistic outlook, whose members saw no fundamental incompatibility between their life as Christians and/or Jews and the surrounding Hellenistic culture. Some similarities to the teaching of the New Testament are apparent, which may indicate its influence on this text, and also illustrates the shared religious and cultural background of these two collections of writings. A particularly clear example of such correspondence is the emphasis on forgiving and doing good to those who wish you harm (see e.g. *T. Gad* 6.3; *T. Jos.* 18.2; *T. Benj.* 4.2–3; cf. *Jos. Asen.* 28.5, 10; cf. Matt. 5.38–47; Luke 6.27–36; Rom. 12.17–21).

The second noticeable theme of the text is its future expectation. Eschatological sections are included in all 12 testaments, and these often overlap or show some stereotypical features, yet they reveal a variety of perspectives which are allowed to co-exist. Four main types of future hope can be identified. First, there are passages in which the patriarch is presented as foretelling the future sins of his descendants, which will result in their exile but eventual restoration by God (see e.g. *T. Levi* 10.1–5; 14.1—16.5; *T. Jud.* 23.1–5; *T. Iss.* 6.1–4; *T. Zeb.* 9.5–7; *T. Dan* 5.6–9; *T. Naph.* 4.1–3; *T. Ash.* 7.2–7; *T. Benj.* 9.1–3). Second, the resurrection of the patriarch and rule over his tribe in the end times is sometimes envisaged (see e.g. *T. Jud.* 25.1; *T. Zeb.* 10.2; *T. Benj.* 10.7; cf. *T. Sim.* 6.7). Third, the coming of an ideal saviour is awaited (see e.g. *T. Levi* 18.1–14; *T. Jud.* 24.1–6; *T. Zeb.* 9.8; *T. Dan* 5.10–13; *T. Naph.* 4.5), in language often reflecting Christian claims about Jesus. Finally, Levi and Judah are frequently exalted, and a special role for their descendants in the future predicted (see e.g. *T. Reu.* 6.5–12; *T. Sim.* 5.4–6; 7.1–2; *T. Levi* 2.11; *T. Iss.* 5.7–8; *T. Dan* 5.4; *T. Naph.* 5.2–6; 8.2; *T. Gad* 8.1).

No clear and unified picture of future salvation emerges from this text, then. Thus, some passages seem to foretell the advent of two figures, a Levitical high priest and a king from the tribe of Judah (*T. Sim.* 7.2), but others only one, variously an ideal priest (*T. Levi* 18.2–13), a star from Jacob (*T. Jud.* 24.1), an eschatological prophet (*T. Benj.* 9.2) or a saviour descended from both Levi and Judah (*T. Dan* 5.10). In general (with the exception of *T. Naph.* 8.2), Levi is regarded as more important than Judah, with even Judah presented as telling his children to recognize that the kingship given to their tribe is subject to the priesthood accorded to Levi and his descendants (*T. Jud.* 21.2–4). He is specifically associated with heavenly matters (*T. Jud.* 21.3–4) and divine revelation (*T. Levi* 2.3—3.8), and attributes traditionally associated with the Davidic kings are here ascribed to Levi and his descendants, such as the spirit of understanding promised to the shoot of Jesse (*T. Levi* 2.3; cf. Isa. 11.2).

The individual testaments highlight different aspects of Levi's leadership, describing him, for example, as the interpreter of the law (cf. Deut. 33.10) and king as well as a priest in *Testament of Reuben* 6.5–12, but as a warrior leader in *Testament of Simeon* 5.5. A focus on the significance of his role as the first priest is a common thread throughout the work, however, an emphasis which may indicate that the *Testaments of the Twelve Patriarchs*, or at least the sources on which it draws, had a high regard for the priesthood. The *Testament of Levi* chapters 14—17 in particular assures its readers that God will intervene to correct the current abuses within that institution, which culminated in the involvement of priests in the rejection and death of Jesus, and will then send the people a new priest who will bring true peace and enlightenment (*T. Levi* 18.2–5).

The *Testaments of the Twelve Patriarchs* is also interesting because of the exegetical traditions which it preserves. This feature of the text is increasingly being recognized by commentators, and is likely to continue as a particular focus of scholarly interest.[2] For example, many of the additional details given here about the lives of the patriarchs answer questions or clarify possible ambiguities raised by the underlying scriptural narrative. It is, for example, made clear in the *Testament of Reuben* that Bilhah was not in any sense to blame for his sexual act with her, since she was bathing in a sheltered place when he first saw her, not drawing attention to herself, and then she slept through it all (*T. Reu.* 3.11–14; cf. Gen. 35.22). Levi's slaughter of the Shechemites is also given additional justification by the claim that he knew that they were intending to capture and rape Sarah and Rebecca just as they had Dinah (*T. Levi* 6.9).

The history of interpretation is further evident in the attachment of differing amounts of guilt to Joseph's brothers for their part in selling him to the Ishmaelites. Dan and Gad, for instance, are said to have particularly hated their brother (*T. Dan* 1.4–8; *T. Gad* 2.1–4; cf. Gen. 37.2), and a similar tradition may be reflected in *Joseph and Aseneth* 24.1—25.8. Joseph is a central figure throughout the whole work, and no part of the Genesis story which might reflect badly on him is ever alluded to, such as his boasting about his dreams of greatness (Gen. 37.5–11) or his rather ambiguous treatment of his brothers when they arrive in Egypt (Gen. 42—44). On the contrary, the *Testament of Joseph* claims that he showed them only kindness and compassion at that time, despite their past envy of him, and that he refused to exalt himself over them, his grand position at Pharaoh's court notwithstanding (see especially *T. Jos.* 17.1–8). The author also stresses the lengths to which Joseph went in order to avoid bringing shame on them, refusing, even under threat of

---

[2] See e.g. R. A. Kugler, *The Testaments of the Twelve Patriarchs.* 2001, Sheffield: Sheffield Academic Press.

punishment, to admit to his Ishmaelite captors that he was not really a slave but had been sold by his own brothers, for example (*T. Jos.* 10.6; 11.2; 13.9; 17.1; cf. 16.5).

Several of the other testaments depict the patriarchs as urging their children to 'pattern your life after the good and pious man Joseph'[3] (*T. Benj.* 3.1), following especially his example of self-control (e.g. *T. Reu.* 4.8–10; cf. *T. Jos.* 8.2; 10.2), compassion (*T. Zeb.* 8.4) and brotherly love (*T. Sim.* 4.4–6). Joseph's great virtue and achievements are widely celebrated in early Jewish literature, not least in *Joseph and Aseneth* (see above, Chapter 3) and also in the *Aramaic Levi Document* to which the *Testament of Levi* is related, so this idealized representation of him is not unusual. It may, however, reflect the Christian influence on the final shaping of the *Testaments of the Twelve Patriarchs*, too, since Joseph has perhaps become a kind of prototype of Jesus, who would also perfectly exemplify the virtues of forbearance under trial and forgiveness.

This text also places a noteworthy emphasis on the effectiveness of intercession, like other writings discussed later in this chapter, namely the *Testament of Moses* and the *Testament of Abraham*, and some apocalyptic texts, such as *4 Ezra* (see below, Chapter 6). In acknowledging the seriousness of his sin with Bilhah, for instance, Reuben says: 'if my father, Jacob, had not prayed to the Lord on my behalf, the Lord would have destroyed me' (*T. Reu.* 1.7; cf. 4.4; cf. *T. Levi* 15.4; *T. Naph.* 6.8; *T. Gad* 5.9). Angels are also pictured interceding for human beings in heaven (*T. Levi* 3.5; 5.6). Finally, Satan, more usually termed here Beliar, is a reality for the authors of the *Testaments of the Twelve Patriarchs*, and evil or deceitful spirits are assumed to lead people astray to commit sin (see e.g. *T. Reu.* 3.1–8; 4.7–9; *T. Sim.* 3.1; *T. Jud.* 14.8; *T. Iss.* 7.7; *T. Zeb.* 9.7; *T. Dan* 1.7; 5.6; *T. Ash.* 6.5; *T. Benj.* 3.3).

Overall, it is very interesting to see how this final Christian form of the *Testaments of the Twelve Patriarchs* holds together adherence to the teachings of Israel's patriarchs, to the moral norms of the Graeco-Roman world and to belief in Jesus as saviour. It is possible, therefore, that it emerged from within early Christian communities

---

[3] All translations of the text are taken from H. C. Kee, 'Testaments of the Twelve Patriarchs'. In *The Old Testament Pseudepigrapha Vol. 1*. Ed. J. H. Charlesworth. 1983, New York: Doubleday, pp. 775–828.

concerned about either the ongoing relevance for them of the Jewish Scriptures and/or the fate of the people of Israel in God's plan of salvation (cf. Rom. 9—11). Its final authors apparently understood faith in Jesus as being entirely consistent with Jewish beliefs and traditions, and may have had potential Jewish converts as well as Christian readers in view in claiming that the future saviour 'will save all the gentiles and the tribe of Israel' (*T. Sim.* 7.2; cf. *T. Benj.* 10.11).[4]

The *Testament of Job*

Introduction to the *Testament of Job*

The narrative setting for this work is the final days of the life of Job. In typical testamentary form, Job is pictured as wanting to settle his affairs before he dies. He therefore calls his children to him (1.2) and relates his life story, focusing especially on his many years of undeserved suffering and loss. Throughout this lengthy speech, he commends to his descendants the virtue of endurance which he has demonstrated so fully himself. The dialogue between Job and his three friends familiar from Scripture is reflected here (chapters 28—43), but the substance and tone of these exchanges are very different, and the *Testament of Job* as a whole expands considerably on the canonical version. Job has an initial encounter with a heavenly messenger (chapters 2—5), for instance, and there is a detailed description of the precious inheritance which he gives to his daughters (chapters 46—50).

The text survives only in a small number of mediaeval Greek and Slavonic manuscripts, and an incomplete Coptic version dating from the fifth century CE. It was probably composed originally in Greek, since it reflects both the language and contents of the Septuagint translation of the biblical book of Job, which differs somewhat from the form in the Hebrew Bible. The emphasis on Job's wealth, piety and generosity in the *Testament of Job* echoes chapters 29—31 of the Septuagint text, for instance. Some of these similarities may be due to the use of common traditions, or the literary influence could

---

[4] See e.g. M. de Jonge, 'The Future of Israel in the Testaments of the Twelve Patriarchs'. *JSJ* 17 (1986), pp. 196–211.

have worked both ways, with later versions of the Septuagint being influenced by this narrative. The names of Job's daughters also follow the Septuagint, and reflect the influence of Hellenistic culture, with one being called Amaltheia's Horn or 'Horn of Plenty', for example.

There is no firm evidence about when and where the *Testament of Job* was written, so it is usually dated to the first century CE, or possibly the first century BCE. Its composition may reflect a time when some Diaspora Jewish communities were facing persecution or a loss of social status, and so needed encouragement to endure their difficulties as steadfastly as Job.[5] Several commentators argue for an Egyptian provenance, mainly because the text identifies Job as king of Egypt (28.7; see also 3.7; 20.4; 29.3; 31.5; 32.2–12), perhaps drawing this inference from the designation of his friends as kings in the Septuagint (Job 2.11). There are no features which would link the *Testament of Job* definitively with any particular religious party like the Pharisees or Essenes. Since it was preserved and transmitted by early Christians and contains very few specifically Jewish features, Christian authorship, or Christian editing of an earlier Jewish source, cannot be ruled out entirely, although it is widely accepted as a Jewish writing. Maria Haralambakis has recently explained the continuing interest of Christians in it as indicating that it was read as a kind of life story of a saint, at a time when hagiographical writings were very popular.[6]

Key features of the *Testament of Job*

The *Testament of Job* clearly fits within the genre of a farewell discourse given by an important scriptural figure to his children. However, this deathbed setting is alluded to only briefly and occasionally (see 1.2–7; 5.1; 6.1; 9.1; 27.7; 45.1), and, despite the text's emphasis on the virtue of endurance, there is less ethical exhortation than in some other works of this type, such as the *Testaments of the Twelve Patriarchs*. Eschatological expectation is not very prominent, either,

---

[5] This is the view of e.g. John Collins; see his 'Structure and Meaning in the Testament of Job'. In *Society of Biblical Literature 1974 Seminar Papers*. Ed. G. MacRae. 1974, Cambridge, Massachusetts: SBL, Vol. 1, pp. 33–52.

[6] See M. Haralambakis, *The Testament of Job: Text, Narrative and Reception History*. 2012, London: T&T Clark.

although there are some apocalyptic features, including Job's claim that he received a divine revelation about future events (47.9). Apart from the testamentary framework, the text offers a very strong and engaging story line, developing the dramatic aspects already present in the biblical account of the life of Job. His complete reversal of fortune is ironically illustrated, for example, by showing how he moved from his royal throne to a seat on top of a dung heap (20.7; 21.1; cf. 32.1–12), and the narrative's leading characters are developed into well-rounded and sympathetic figures. The readers can feel, for instance, Job's real sorrow at the loss of his children (19.1–2) and be moved by the hardships and sacrifices borne by his wife during his long years of poverty and illness (chapters 21—23).

The *Testament of Job* shares some of the features characteristic of biblical expansions and rewritten Bible texts in the way it builds on the scriptural story of Job. So, for example, minor female characters like his first wife Sitidos (or Sitis) are named and given a more prominent voice. Precise dates and timings provide information about matters such as the length of time that Job was afflicted with plague (21.1; 26.1), or that his friends sat arguing with him (41.1). The author also takes an interest in numbers, often seeking to augment Job's wealth and status by attributing to him far more possessions and livestock than the underlying biblical text. His sheep are said to have totalled 130,000 before he lost them, for instance (9.1; cf. the figure of 7,000 in Job 1.3), and it is claimed that in his house he had 30 (10.1) or even 60 (32.7) tables of food constantly prepared for strangers.

A further interesting feature of this work is the inclusion of several carefully crafted poetic laments (25.1–8; 32.1–12; 43.4–17; cf. 53.2–4), which often employ a repeated refrain (e.g. 25.1–8; 32.1–12). Reference is made also to the existence of other collections of hymns, including some composed by Job's daughters (40.14; 49.2; 50.3; 51.4; cf. 40.14; 41.6). The creation of new songs and prayers has been identified throughout this volume as a noteworthy feature of the writings of the Second Temple period; these often serve as a vehicle for theological teaching and may also indicate the importance of hymns in the Jewish worship of the time. Another literary form incorporated into the *Testament of Job* is the riddle (see especially chapters 36 and 38), a feature of the canonical book of Job and both wisdom and apocalyptic writings more generally, such as *4 Ezra* (see further below, Chapter 6).

Important themes in the *Testament of Job*

One of the most significant differences between the *Testament of Job* and the scriptural account of Job's life is that his afflictions are explained throughout as resulting directly from his decision to destroy a pagan temple near his home after realizing that idol worship is useless and diabolic (2.1—3.7). He is undeterred from taking this action even though he is warned beforehand by an angel of the consequences: 'If you attempt to purge the place of Satan, he will rise up against you with wrath for battle . . . he will bring on you many plagues, he will take away for himself your goods, he will carry off your children' (4.4–5).[7] This interpretation provides a more satisfying explanation for Job's suffering than the idea that he was used as a kind of pawn to enable God to prove a point to Satan (Job 2.1–6), and it leads to a serious shift in the presentation of Job: he is no longer simply an innocent man who endures undeserved afflictions righteously but passively. Instead he is transformed into a brave hero who consciously and actively takes on the power of Satan, calling on him, for example, to: 'Stop hiding yourself! . . . Come out and fight!' (27.1). Through his encounter with the heavenly messenger, Job also becomes the recipient of revealed knowledge, gaining an understanding of the real meaning of events which is denied to all the other characters in the narrative (3.1—4.11).

The *Testament of Job* does not function, then, like its canonical namesake, as an attempt to wrestle with the theological problem of innocent suffering, but rather as an exhortation to steadfastly endure sorrow and difficulties in the well-founded hope of eventual reward, for the angel promises Job:

> But if you are patient, I will make your name renowned in all generations of the earth . . . And I will return you again to your goods. It will be repaid to you doubly . . . And you shall be raised up in the resurrection . . . (4.6–9; cf. 18.5–8)

---

[7] All translations of the text are taken from R. P. Spittler, 'Testament of Job'. In *The Old Testament Pseudepigrapha Vol. 1*. Ed. J. H. Charlesworth. 1983, New York: Doubleday, pp. 829–68.

In this version of events, Satan also has a more active and prominent role, so that he does not simply receive from God limited and temporary power (Job 2.6) to harm Job, but wages a long-running and destructive campaign against him. The death of Job's children, and the loss of his house and possessions, is directly attributed to Satan, not to a wind as in Scripture (17.6—18.1; cf. Job 1.19), for example, and Satan is also accused of being the inspiration for the words of Job's wife and his friend Elihu when they try to persuade him to give up and denounce God (26.6; 41.5).

Satan is presented above all as a deceiver (3.3) who, in order to trick human beings, can adopt various disguises, such as a beggar (6.4), a bread seller (23.1) and a foreign king (17.20). The warning to the readers, then, is that Satan can appear in many forms and will seduce all but those who have insight and are on their guard. A similar portrayal of the devil is found in *The Life of Adam and Eve* (see Chapter 3, above) where he also surfaces in different guises and is the enemy of human beings (as in *T. Job* 47.10), constantly seeking to deceive and ensnare them.

This narrative of the contest between Job and Satan brings into focus the hero's fortitude. From the outset, Job describes himself as one 'fully engaged in endurance' (1.5), and several times he reiterates his willingness to bear whatever trials befall him (5.1; 7.13; 26.4–5). He might be regarded as taking this attitude to extremes, going so far, for instance, as to put straight back on to his worm-ridden body any parasite which crawled off it (20.8–9)! Ultimately, this virtue brings about his victory over Satan, who withdraws from his struggle with Job, wearied by his perseverance (27.2–5). This emphasis is something of a development of the biblical figure of Job, who, while he does remain faithful in suffering, does not always do so in patient endurance, but rather openly questions God and even curses the day of his birth (e.g. Job 3.1–26). It is, however, Job's steadfastness which is particularly highlighted in later interpretation, so that, for example, this quality is mentioned in the only New Testament reference to him (Jas. 5.11).

His charity towards the needy and strangers is also a noteworthy theme of the *Testament of Job* (see especially chapters 9—13; cf. Job 29.12–16; 32.1–12), with the mourners at his funeral lamenting: 'Gone is the father of the orphans! Gone is the host of strangers!

Gone is the clothing of widows! Who then will not weep over the man of God?' (53.3–4). This portrayal may well reflect an exegetical tendency to draw comparisons between Job and Abraham, another biblical figure renowned for his faithfulness and hospitality. According to some traditions, for instance, Abraham, like the Job of this text, destroyed a pagan temple near his home when he became convinced of the foolishness of idolatry (*Jub.* 12.12).[8] Job is specifically connected with the family of Abraham here by the claim that his second wife and the mother of his surviving children is Dinah, the daughter of Jacob and Leah (1.6; cf. *L.A.B.* 8.7–8; *Targum Job* 2.9; *Genesis Rabbah* 57.4).

There are also some similarities between this Job and Tobit, as both are generous almsgivers who endure difficult times without complaint, and become dependent for a time on the financial support of their wives (Tobit 2.11; cf. *T. Job* 21.2). It is these virtues of patient endurance and charity which Job commends to his children (27.7; 45.2). He also encourages them to look beyond worthless earthly goods to the far more glorious heavenly reward which awaits the faithful, and which is pictured as both an everlasting heavenly throne (33.2–9) and a wealthy and splendid city (18.5–8): 'I also considered my goods as nothing compared to the city about which the angel spoke to me' (18.8). Similar sentiments are expressed elsewhere in Jewish literature, as well as in the New Testament (see, for example, the discussion of *Jos. Asen.* 12.15 in Chapter 3, above). There are no lists of vices or lengthy warnings against immorality in this narrative, unlike some other examples of the testament genre. The only negative instruction given by the dying Job to his descendants is to avoid intermarriage with strangers (45.3), although elsewhere the sins of pride (15.8) and arrogance and boastfulness (21.3; 33.8) are also condemned.

The discussion of the *Testament of Job* to this point has referred several times to its women characters, whose strikingly prominent place in the narrative has generated considerable scholarly discussion. The first woman to feature is an unnamed door-maid, who disobeys Job's instructions and gives a loaf of bread to Satan when he comes

---

[8] For further detail about the frequent juxtaposition of Job and Abraham in early Jewish interpretation, see D. C. Allison, 'Job in the *Testament of Abraham*'. *JSP* 12 (2001), pp. 131–47.

to the house disguised as a beggar (6.1—7.13). A substantial portion of the text (chapters 21—25) is then devoted to describing how Job's wife Sitidos is affected by his illness and loss of wealth. She has to work as a servant for years to support Job, even turning to begging, eventually enduring the public humiliation of having her head shaved so that she might sell her hair to buy bread. Unfortunately, she, like the door-maid, is tricked into this course of action by Satan in disguise (23.1–11), and then, unable to bear her misfortunes any longer, she calls on Job to free them both from their pain by speaking a word against God so that they might die (25.10; cf. Job 2.9).

Both of these women have positive characteristics: the door-maid is motivated by kindness and a concern for her master's reputation for almsgiving, and Sitidos proves herself to be very loyal to her husband and capable of great self-sacrifice. On the other hand, neither of them has any insight into the real meaning of Job's suffering, and they are ultimately unable to remain faithful when tested by Satan, partly because they are too concerned with how they appear in the eyes of other people. That the devil is able to deceive them both with his disguises and clever words may reflect a view that women are more susceptible than men to such seduction (see also the discussion of *The Life of Adam and Eve* in Chapter 3 above; cf. *T. Reu.* 5.3; *T. Jud.* 15.5–6). It should be noted, however, that several men in the story are likewise taken in by Satan and become his instruments, including many of the citizens of Job's country (17.2) and his friend Elihu (41.5).

A further clue to understanding the role of women in the *Testament of Job* is to be found in the remarkable account of the dying Job giving his three daughters an inheritance better than that of their seven brothers (chapters 46—50). Since the underlying scriptural narrative states that his daughters inherited alongside their male relatives (Job 42.15), it is possible that later interpreters felt a need to explain a situation which would have been unusual in the ancient world. Here, this legacy is specified: it is not money or lands, which were properly assigned only to Job's sons (46.1), but three multicoloured cords, which are to be worn like a sash (46.9). These cords appear insignificant on first sight, but in fact they have an inestimable value, as they were given to Job directly by God (47.4–5), possess healing powers (47.6), protect against evil (47.11) and are almost magical in appearance: 'they were not from the earth but from heaven, shimmering with fiery sparks like the rays of the sun' (46.8). It is possible that they deliberately recall the colourful breastplate or special clothes worn by the Jewish high priests when they officiated in the sanctuary (e.g. Exod. 28).[9] As soon as each daughter in turn puts on her sash, she goes into an ecstatic state and is able to speak in tongues or the language of the angels (48.1—50.3; cf. 52.7). Unlike most of Job's friends and relatives, they are then able to see their father being taken up into heaven in a gleaming chariot (52.6–9; cf. 47.11). Job's bequest changes their hearts so that they no longer think of earthly things but are led 'into the better world, to live in the heavens' (47.3; cf. 48.2; 49.1; 50.2).

This scene, therefore, reinforces the message of the whole narrative about the superiority of everlasting heavenly reward over the transience of earthly wealth and honour.[10] The role played by the three daughters in these chapters is so significant that some commentators have tried to link the text, or at least this section of it, to groups which are thought to have allowed women a leading role in worship, or which valued prophecy or healing powers. It has thus been associated with sects as diverse as the Egyptian Jewish Therapeutae[11] and the second-century Christian Montanists.[12] These theories have attracted few followers, however, and the theological and ethical teaching of the *Testament of Job* does not stand out as remarkable from the thought of Hellenistic Judaism in general, sharing, for example, the widespread tendency to criticize idolatry and promote generosity to the poor. Nevertheless, if it is not a Christian composition, it serves as a further witness to the diversity of belief and liturgical practice which characterized Second Temple Judaism, indicating a

---

[9] E.g. a recent study by Jennifer Zilm has drawn attention to the use of a similar motif of multicoloured threads in the Qumran liturgical text the *Songs of the Sabbath Sacrifice*. See her 'Multi-Coloured Like Woven Works: Gender, Ritual Clothing and Praying with the Angels in the Dead Sea Scrolls and the Testament of Job'. In *Prayer and Poetry in the Dead Sea Scrolls and Related Literature. Essays in Honour of Eileen Schuller on the Occasion of Her 65th Birthday.* Ed. J. Penner, K. M. Penner and C. Wassen. 2012, Leiden: Brill, pp. 437-51.

[10] This point is stressed especially in R. A. Kugler and R.L. Rohrbaugh, 'On Women and Honour in the *Testament of Job*'. *JSP* 14 (2004), pp. 43–62.

[11] See M. Philonenko, 'Le Testament de Job et les Thérapeutes'. *Semitica* 8 (1958), pp. 41–53.

[12] See R. P. Spittler, 'The Testament of Job: A History of Research and Interpretation'. In *Studies on the Testament of Job.* Ed. M. A. Knibb and P. W. van der Horst. 1989, Cambridge: Cambridge University Press, pp. 7–32.

wider interest in glossolalia and the possibility of mystical communication with angels similar to that reflected in the Qumran *Songs of the Sabbath Sacrifices.*

The *Testament of Moses*

Introduction to the *Testament of Moses*

This text presents itself as the farewell speech of Moses to his divinely appointed successor, Joshua (1.6). Its scriptural starting point, therefore, is the end of the book of Deuteronomy (chapters 31—34; see especially Deut. 31.7–8, 14–24; 34.1–9). The author rewrites this account of Moses' last words in order to provide a theological lesson for his contemporaries. He has Moses foretell in summary form the history of Israel (cf. Deut. 31.16–21) from the conquest of Canaan up to his own time (chapters 2—6), and then predict the trials associated with the coming eschatological age (chapters 7—9). This historical review highlights a repeated pattern of sinfulness and infidelity on the part of the people, but also assures the audience of their eventual restoration by God: 'For God Most High will surge forth ... he will come to work vengeance on the nations ... Then will you be happy, O Israel! And you will mount up above the necks and the wings of an eagle' (10.7–8).[13]

A number of specific historical references within the work help to date it. Chapter 6, for example, contains clear allusions to the 34-year-long reign of Herod the Great (37–4 BCE; see 6.2–6), to his sons (6.7), and to a partial destruction of the Temple soon after his death (6.9), reflecting the events of 4 BCE, when the Roman general Varus suppressed a rebellion in Jerusalem. This would indicate that the *Testament of Moses* was written in the early decades of the first century CE, probably before the destruction of Jerusalem in 70 CE, since the continued existence of the Temple seems to be assumed (e.g. 1.17; 5.4).

There are, however, some echoes of what is known of the reign of the cruel Antiochus IV Epiphanes (175–164 BCE) in the description in chapter 8 of a time of great suffering and persecution for

---

[13] All translations of the text are taken from J. Priest, 'Testament of Moses'. In *The Old Testament Pseudepigrapha Vol. 1.* Ed. J. H. Charlesworth. 1983, New York: Doubleday, pp. 919–34.

the people of Israel. Several commentators, therefore, argue that the majority of the *Testament of Moses* was composed in the mid-second century BCE as a response to the events of this time, then was later revised and updated for a new context with the addition of chapter 6 (and perhaps also chapters 5 and/or 7).[14] Apocalyptic predictions and prophetic oracles certainly were often adapted and applied to new circumstances, as was the case, for instance, with the sibylline literature (discussed above in Chapter 4) and in *1 Enoch* (see further below, Chapter 6). On the other hand, these warnings are rather vague and stereotypical, and do not necessarily reflect only the time of Antiochus IV: as was noted in relation to the *Sibylline Oracles*, later authors could draw on traditions associated with hated figures of the past like Antiochus or Herod for their descriptions of the tribulations of the final age. The book also reads plausibly as a literary unity. In its present form, then, the *Testament of Moses* definitely dates from the first century CE, but the extent to which it includes older material remains uncertain. Like the *Psalms of Solomon* (see above, Chapter 4), it is concerned almost exclusively with events in Jerusalem and Judaea, so was very probably composed in that region.

There is just one extant manuscript of the *Testament of Moses*, dating from the sixth century CE. This was only discovered in 1861, in the Ambrosian Library in Milan. It is written in Latin, but is almost certainly a translation from Greek. It is often suggested that a Hebrew or Aramaic original underlies the Greek version, on the basis of some perceived Semitisms in the text's language and syntax, but the evidence for this is debatable.[15] If it was composed in Greek and in a Judaean context, it offers interesting evidence for the extent to which the Greek language was used by Palestinian as well as Diaspora Jews in this era. Unfortunately, this single manuscript is fragmentary, so large sections of the work are missing, including its ending. It is therefore impossible to be certain whether it originally concluded with an account of Moses' death and burial, a typical

---

[14] This view is particularly associated with George Nickelsburg; see e.g. his *Jewish Literature between the Bible and the Mishnah*. 2nd edn. 2005, Minneapolis: Fortress Press, pp. 74–6, 247–8.

[15] One of the most thorough recent studies of this question concludes that a Hebrew original is very unlikely; see J. Tromp, *The Assumption of Moses: A Critical Edition with Commentary*. 1993, Leiden; Brill, pp. 78–85.

feature of the testament form. The work is also known as the *Assumption of Moses*, because when it was first unearthed, it was identified with a lost writing of that name referred to in early church sources. 'Testament' is a better title than 'Assumption', however, because the text in its current form does not describe Moses dying and being taken up to heaven, but is presented as his last words or testament.

Key features of the *Testament of Moses*

This is another example of a work which could be assigned to more than one literary genre. It is framed as a testamentary speech, although it does not include as much ethical exhortation as, for instance, the *Testaments of the Twelve Patriarchs*. It could also be viewed, at least to some extent, as a rewriting or expansion of Deuteronomy chapters 31—34, the scriptural account of Moses' farewell and death, to which it specifically refers (1.5). In addition, it is often classified as an apocalyptic writing, because it includes an eschatological section (chapters 8—10), looking forward to a glorious future for Israel and the destruction of its enemies. Like many apocalypses, it also includes a review of history, divided into periods (2.3–6; 10.12–13; cf. *1 En.* 93.3–14; 91.12–17), and chapter 10 takes the form of an eschatological song. The importance of hymns in the literature of the Second Temple period in general has been noted repeatedly in this volume, and there are several specific instances of songs or poems being used as the vehicle for expressions of eschatological hope (e.g. Tobit 13; *1 En.* 96; *Pss. Sol.* 11). The final chapters of Deuteronomy may well have provided the primary inspiration for this hymn, however, since it contains clear allusions to the two songs predicting Israel's ultimate vindication which Moses is said to have uttered there (see e.g. Deut. 31.30—32.43; 33.1–29).

Important themes in the *Testament of Moses*

Moses is a towering figure in the Jewish literature of this period, eulogized by writers like Artapanus, Josephus and Philo as the ultimate legislator, original philosopher, ideal king and most brilliant of military commanders. This author, however, chooses to call Moses a prophet (11.16; cf. 1.5) and to emphasize his role as a mediator between God and the people of Israel (1.14; 11.17; cf. 11.11; cf. *L.A.B.* 19.3). This understanding of Moses is rooted in the book of

Deuteronomy (see e.g. Deut. 9.18–29; 10.10; 18.15–18; 34.10). The reality of his death in the presence of all the people' (1.15; cf. 11.5–8) is also stressed, possibly in response to contemporary debates about this question, given that the place of his burial was unknown (Deut. 34.6; see, for example, the discussion in Chapter 2 above of *L.A.B.* 19.16; cf. Jude 9).

Moses is described in particularly glowing terms in one verse as: 'that sacred spirit, worthy of the Lord, manifold and incomprehensible, master of the word, faithful in all things, the divine prophet for the whole earth, the perfect teacher in the world' (11.16). Nevertheless, he is not idealized to the same degree as in other early Jewish writings, and it is even expressly stated that his successes in protecting and interceding for the people are 'not on account of . . . my strength, (it is) simply that his [i.e. God's] mercies and long-suffering have lighted on me' (12.7). This is primarily because the author's focus is not on the person or life of Moses *per se* as much as on the teaching which he seeks to convey through the final speech which he attributes to him. Above all, he reassures his audience that, if they obey the commandments (12.10), God will remain faithful to the covenant, and will ultimately intervene decisively on behalf of the chosen people of Israel.

This message is directed to a society which is perceived to be in crisis, reflecting the fact that at least the final form of the *Testament of Moses* was composed in the turbulent years of the early first century CE. The ruling classes in particular are heavily criticized for their corruption, hypocrisy and lack of concern for the poor (e.g. 7.1–10; cf. *1 En.* 62.3–12). Parts of the text seem to imply a rejection of the Hasmonaean priests and the cult of the Second Temple as defiled and polluted by idolatry: 'Then powerful kings will rise over them, and they will be called priests of the Most High God. They will perform great impiety in the Holy of Holies' (6.1; cf. 4.8; 5.3–5). All these accusations share a similar spirit with the *Psalms of Solomon* (see above, Chapter 4) and some of the Qumran Scrolls, which were written at about this time. However, the evil behaviour of these kings and priests is presented as part of a pattern of idolatry and unfaithfulness to God which has characterized the Israelites throughout their history, something which Moses predicted (e.g. 2.7–9) and of which God had complete foreknowledge (12.4–5, 13).

Such sinfulness leads to divine punishment, as at the time of the exile (3.1–3), but when the people repent (e.g. 3.4–13), they are forgiven and restored: 'Then God will remember them because of the covenant which he made with their fathers and will openly show his compassion' (4.5).

An interesting aspect of the theology of the *Testament of Moses* is its emphasis on the role played by the effective intercession of Israel's leaders, like Moses, in moving God to intervene to save the people (e.g. 4.1–6; 11.17; cf. 9.1–7). The possibility of mercy and restoration is, therefore, signalled by the historical review, but is further reinforced in the final words of comfort which Moses speaks to his successor, Joshua, who is concerned that he will not be able to guide and protect the community as effectively as Moses did (11.9–19). Moses assures him that God is in absolute control of all events and will never allow the people to be extinguished (12.12).

Throughout, God's special relationship with Israel is emphasized, in a way which echoes the outlook of writings like *Jubilees* and the *Biblical Antiquities* (see above, Chapter 2). So, for example, the text claims that the world was created on Israel's behalf (1.12; cf. *4 Ezra* 6.55, 59; 7.11; *2 Bar.* 14.19); that their land is given to them by God's promise and oath (1.9; cf. 2.1); that God is constantly faithful to the covenant made with them (e.g. 1.8–9; 3.9; 4.2–6; 10.15; 11.17; 12.13); and that they can expect to be raised to heaven in the future to rejoice over their enemies (10.7–10). The gentile nations, on the other hand, are guilty of practising idolatry and failing to understand the real meaning of creation (1.13; 10.7). The author's deterministic outlook, with its assumptions about divine foresight and government, leads him to conclude that God must have deliberately hidden true knowledge about the world and its purpose from the gentiles, favouring only Israel with such understanding: 'he did not make this purpose of creation openly known from the beginning of the world so that the nations might be found guilty' (1.12–13). This seems to be an interesting theological development of the scriptural idea that God deliberately 'hardened the hearts' of Israel's enemies (e.g. Exod. 4.21; 7.3; 9.12; 10.1–27; 11.10; 14.4, 8; cf. Isa. 6.9–10).

Israel's restoration to glory would probably have seemed an unlikely prospect at the time the *Testament of Moses* was written, whether in the late second century BCE or early first century CE. The author insists, however, that this will come about in the eschatological future, and includes a song celebrating the imminent appearance of God on earth (10.3), to defeat the devil (10.1), punish the nation's adversaries (10.7), establish the reign of God throughout all Creation (10.1) and exalt the Israelites above the gentiles to dwell in heaven (10.8–10). In this picture of the end times, it is God who intervenes directly and decisively on behalf of the covenant people (e.g. 10.3, 7, 9), so there is no unambiguous reference to any other saviour.

Two figures are associated in the text with Israel's vindication, however, and are, therefore, possibly to be regarded as having messianic functions. The first is a heavenly messenger who plays some part in God's enacting of vengeance on Israel's enemies (10.2). He is not named, and his role is not clearly outlined, making him difficult to identify. The most natural explanation is that he is an angel, perhaps Israel's guardian or patron angel Michael. However, it is said of him that, at the appointed time, his 'hands will be filled', a term generally used for priestly ordination, so the appearance of a future ideal priest (cf. *T. Levi* 18.1–14) may be envisaged. Given the emphasis throughout the *Testament of Moses* on the theme of intercession, it has also been suggested this figure should be understood as a mediator, one who conveys the cries of the suffering people to God (cf. 4.1–4), either an angel, or even perhaps Moses himself, advocating on their behalf in heaven as he did on earth.[16]

Second, a Levite called Taxo is introduced rather enigmatically in chapter 9. He is described as being so exercised by the punishment and suffering which the people of Israel are enduring that he decides to fast for three days and then retreat into a cave in the desert with his seven sons. There, they resolve to die rather than transgress the commandments, 'For if we do this, and do die, our blood will be avenged before the Lord' (9.6–7). These verses have provoked a great deal of scholarly discussion, but to date no real consensus has emerged as to the meaning of either Taxo's actions or his unusual name. Various attempts have been made, sometimes using devices such as gematria, to identify him with a known historical person, such as Mattathias, the father of the Maccabees, or the rebel leader

---

[16] For this interpretation, see W. J. van Henten, 'Moses as Heavenly Messenger in *Assumptio Mosis* 10:2 and Qumran Passages'. *JJS* 54 (2003), pp. 216–27.

Judas the Galilean (Josephus, *Ant.* 18.1; cf. Acts 5.37), but it is more likely that he is to be understood as an ideal figure. Similarly, many explanations of his name have been put forward, but none is entirely convincing. The most widely accepted suggestions are that it is derived either from a Greek verb meaning 'to prepare' or 'to order'. Taxo is then understood as fulfilling the role of the forerunner of the Messiah, or as one who 'orders' or perhaps even 'interprets' events or the law.

Even more intriguing is the question of the relationship between Taxo's willingness to die in the desert and the eschatological intervention described in the following chapter. Some commentators argue that the death of the righteous Taxo and his sons is to be understood as providing the catalyst for Israel's salvation, since it prompts God to avenge the innocent suffering of those who remain faithful to the covenant (9.7; 10.2; cf. Deut. 32.43). Johannes Tromp, for instance, has gone so far as to suggest that Taxo and the heavenly messenger of 10.2 are one and the same.[17] This would obviously offer extremely interesting comparative material for early Christian teaching about the sinless Jesus' willingness to accept death on behalf of others. This interpretation cannot be established with certainty, since the text does not make this link explicit, nor even state clearly whether Taxo and his sons did actually die. However, this complex of ideas about the purposeful suffering of the righteous may be at work in both the *Testament of Moses* and the New Testament, especially as stories about martyrs grew in importance and popularity in the Maccabean period (see e.g. 1 Macc. 2 and 2 Macc. 7) and first century CE (e.g. Josephus, *Ant.* 14.15.5). Taxo may also be introduced here to provide a righteous counterpart to Mattathias, as someone who prefers to accept death and leave it to God to avenge his suffering rather than to take up arms against Israel's enemies as the Maccabees did, a choice which is ultimately vindicated. On that reading, which is associated in particular with John Collins,[18] this chapter may attest to a significant pacifist strand within Second Temple Jewish thought.

---

[17] J. Tromp, 'Taxo, the Messenger of the Lord'. *JJS* 21 (1990), pp. 200–9.

[18] J. J. Collins, 'The Date and Provenance of the Testament of Moses'. In *Studies on the Testament of Moses*. Ed. G. W. E. Nickelsburg. 1973, Cambridge, Massachusetts: SBL, pp. 15–32.

The *Testament of Abraham*

Introduction to the *Testament of Abraham*

The *Testament of Abraham* is unlike other examples of this genre because it does not present the final speech of the patriarch Abraham to his gathered descendants, but rather gives an enjoyable fictional account of the events surrounding his death.

The narrative opens with God sending the archangel Michael to earth to warn Abraham that he is about to die and should therefore settle his affairs. Even though he has lived to the astonishingly ripe old age of 995 (1.1), even longer than Methuselah (Gen. 5.27), Abraham refuses to accept the idea of his death, choosing to ignore Michael's message, the words of a talking tree (3.2–3) and a portentous dream of his son Isaac (7.1–10). He employs all kinds of delaying tactics to stave off the inevitable, including asking to see the whole created world before he dies (9.6). This request is granted, so Abraham embarks on a tour of the universe in a chariot drawn by angels (10.1–3). God has to intervene to bring the expedition to a premature end, however, because Abraham starts calling down violent punishments on people whom he sees committing sins (10.4–11), so that God becomes alarmed that he will end up destroying most of humanity if he is allowed to carry on! Michael then takes him to the gates of heaven, to see post-mortem judgement in action (chapters 11—14). This vision teaches Abraham compassion for sinners, so he intercedes on their behalf (11.1—14.15). Yet even after this experience Abraham will not go with Michael (15.10; cf. 7.12), so God has to send to him Death personified to finally take him from the earth (16.1–6). Abraham still refuses to go quietly (16.16), asking more stalling questions (17.9–19), and trying to hide from Death, who pursues him around his house (17.1–3) before eventually tricking him into dying (20.9). His body is buried, and his soul taken up into paradise by angels (20.9–14), without him ever having made his last will and testament.

The text has survived in two forms, which probably go back to a common original, since they follow the same basic story line and often agree in wording and content. The longer version will be considered here, because it is regarded by most commentators as closer to the original. The other recension provides a shorter and rather different account of the heavenly judgement scene witnessed by Abraham, and also tends to present him in a slightly more flattering light.

The *Testament of Abraham* was almost certainly composed in Greek, but translations in a number of languages are extant, including Coptic, Arabic, Ethiopic, Slavonic and Romanian. The existing manuscripts largely date from the mediaeval period or later, and it is difficult to be precise about when and where the work was first composed, as it makes no reference to any specific historical events. It is usually assigned a date in the late first century CE, and Egypt is sometimes suggested as a possible location; the evidence for this setting is not strong, but there are some linguistic similarities to other books which are thought to have been written in Egypt, such as Wisdom and *3 Maccabees,* and the rather unusual allusion to judgement after death as involving the weighing of souls rather than deeds (12.13) is paralleled in Egyptian sources like the ancient funerary text the *Book of the Dead.*

The *Testament of Abraham* is another example of a work which cannot be attributed definitely to either Jewish or Christian authorship. It was preserved and transmitted in Christian circles, and in its present form unquestionably shows signs of Christian editing and use of the New Testament (see e.g. 11.2, 10–11; cf. 13.13). It makes no mention of any belief or teaching which might be regarded as specifically Jewish, such as sabbath observance, circumcision or dietary laws. James Davila has, therefore, concluded that there is no reason why the *Testament of Abraham* could not have been written by a Christian in the early centuries CE.[19] The majority of commentators, however, continue to argue for a Jewish origin for the text, mainly because it seems very unlikely that a Christian work dealing with the subject of death would make no reference to the role of Jesus' crucifixion and resurrection in securing eternal life, or would place Abel (13.2) rather than Christ in the role of heavenly judge.

Key features of the *Testament of Abraham*

As already noted, the typical elements of a testament are lacking in this work, including a farewell speech containing ethical instruction.

---

[19] J. R. Davila, *The Provenance of the Pseudepigrapha: Jewish, Christian or Other?* 2005, Leiden: Brill.

Abraham's revelatory tour of heaven and earth, together with the extended judgement scene, are more reminiscent of apocalyptic writings (see further below, Chapter 6), but such visions are included in other texts which fit within the relatively loose category of testaments. This difficulty in classifying the *Testament of Abraham* highlights once again the widespread co-existence of mixed literary forms in the literature of the Second Temple period. There is no doubt, however, that the most striking feature of this narrative is its use of humour and irony. This is seen most clearly in the portrayal of Abraham, who is a far cry from the solid, obedient patriarch of the Scriptures, and who hardly lives up to his reputation as 'friend of God' (1.7; 2.3, 7; 4.7; 8.2; 15.12–14; 16.5, 9; 19.14). This parody of the righteous Abraham is scared of death to the point of foolishness, stubbornly refuses to co-operate with God or God's messenger, and is on the verge of causing chaos on earth with his hard-hearted and overzealous destruction of every sinner he sees.

Comic elements occur similarly in the depiction of the archangel Michael, who, although supposedly the commander-in-chief of the heavenly hosts, proves to be remarkably weak and ineffective in carrying out God's instructions. He is initially reluctant to give Abraham the bad news of his impending death because he doesn't want to upset him (4.6), and then is so confused about what to do when Abraham declines to go with him that he has to keep running back and forth between earth and heaven to check out his next move with God (8.1–3; 9.7; 15.11–15). Even Death personified is shown to be a coward at heart, so that this being from whom human beings shrink starts trembling when called to appear before God (16.3).

The *Testament of Abraham* naturally draws on the book of Genesis in places for its language and themes, making particular use of the account of the patriarch entertaining three angels near the oaks of Mamre (Gen. 18). It goes far beyond the scriptural text, however, rather in the manner of a biblical expansion (see above, Chapter 3), and at times even contradicts it, both in the general picture given of Abraham and in specific details. Sarah is said to be alive at the time of her husband's death (20.6; cf. Gen. 23.1), for example, and Abraham to live to the age of 995, not 175 (1.1; cf. Gen. 25.7), perhaps indicating that ancient interpreters understood such numbers symbolically rather than literally. That the author was also familiar with Hellenistic literature is indicated, by, for example, the story of the angel's tears turning into precious jewels (3.11), a phenomenon reflected in a number of Greek myths, and by the cypress tree which speaks to predict Abraham's death (3.1–3), echoing the accounts of an oak tree at Dodona which was consulted as an oracle according to sources such as Homer.[20]

Important themes in the *Testament of Abraham*

The portrayal of Abraham as a flawed character with humorous foibles and a great reluctance to die is not an end in itself, but serves the main theological purpose of this text, which is to offer an explanation of death and post-mortem judgement. These are indeed important themes to deal with, since death is both inevitable (1.3; 8.9; cf. 19.7) and something which inspires fear in almost everyone, even the blessed Abraham. The *Testament of Abraham* assumes that every individual will have to face judgement, so it is necessary to try to live a righteous life. The 'Two Ways' theme familiar from Scripture (e.g. Deut. 11.26; 30.15; Pss. 1.6; 119.29–30; Prov. 4.18–19; Jer. 21.8) and both Jewish (e.g. Wisd. 5.6–7; 1QS 3.18–25; *1 En.* 94.1–5; *T. Ash.* 1.3–5; *b. Ber.* 28b) and early Christian (e.g. Matt. 7.13–14; *Didache* 106; *Barn.* 18–21; *Apostolic Constitutions* 1—5) sources is employed, for instance, to highlight the idea that many sinners are on the road to eternal destruction (11.1–12). This chapter has strong echoes of the saying in Matthew's Gospel about the narrow gate, so may well be an example of a Christian addition or revision.

The overall message of the text is, however, a very consoling one: life after death is pleasant and peaceful, repentance is possible and efficacious, and God's compassion is greater than many human beings appreciate: 'But I made the world, and I do not want to destroy any one of them' (10.14).[21] During the course of the narrative, for instance, Abraham comes to learn that he was too harsh on those

---

[20] Further details of the parallels with Greek mythology can be found in D. C. Allison, *Testament of Abraham*. 2003, Berlin: de Gruyter; see esp. pp. 109–11, 123–4.

[21] All translations of the text are taken from E. P. Sanders, 'Testament of Abraham'. In *The Old Testament Pseudepigrapha Vol. 1*. Ed. J. H. Charlesworth. 1983, New York: Doubleday, pp. 871–902.

whom he saw engaged in wrongdoing (10.4–11) and that God's judgement is merciful as well as just (14.1–15). The text also ends with a description of the place where the righteous will dwell after death, where 'there is no toil, no grief, no moaning, but peace and exultation and endless life' (20.14).

As part of this exploration of the theme of judgement, an unusually detailed vision of a heavenly court scene (chapters 11—14) forms a major part of the work, particularly in its longer form. In this section, various traditional motifs are brought together, but not systematically harmonized. Thus three different forms of judgement are described: the recording of good and bad deeds in a book (12.7–8, 17; 13.9); testing by fire (12.10; 13.11–13); and weighing deeds (14.10) or souls (12.13). Different levels of judgement are also alluded to: a judgement of individual souls immediately after death, which is said to be carried out by angels and a wondrous figure seated on a throne (11.1—13.3) who is identified with Abel (13.2); a judgement of gentiles by the 12 tribes of Israel (13.6); and the final apocalyptic judgement of God (13.7). Considerable emphasis is placed on the idea that repentance and intercession for the dead are effective in bringing about God's mercy, so that Michael, for example, assures Abraham that: 'It [a soul whose fate was in the balance] was saved through your righteous prayer' (14.8; cf. 14.12–14).

One of the verses within this scene which has occasioned most comment is a statement that those who suffer an untimely death receive no further punishment in the afterlife, so that inviting sudden death on the wicked is counterproductive: 'But those whom I destroy while they are living on the earth, I do not requite in death' (14.15). This verse implies criticism not only of the actions of Abraham within the narrative (10.5–11), but also of the example of scriptural figures such as Moses (Num. 16.1–50), Elijah (2 Kings 1.9–12) and Elisha (2 Kings 2.23–25), who likewise brought about the violent death of their opponents. Some other early Jewish sources (e.g. *1 En.* 22.12–13) reflect the same perspective as the *Testament of Abraham*, and the view that suffering and death can atone for sin and lessen a person's punishment in the world to come is found in parts of the rabbinic literature. It seems, then, that this was a subject of contemporary theological debate, which may throw an interesting light on the discussion between Jesus and his disciples recorded in

Luke's Gospel about whether to call down fire on some unwelcoming Samaritans (Luke 9.51–56).

Angels are pictured as being both numerous and active in the process of heavenly judgement, and two are named and assigned particularly important roles, Dokiel who weighs and Puriel who tests by fire (13.10–11). Like the archangel Michael, these heavenly beings are described as marvellous in appearance, handsome, youthful and shining brightly like the sun (2.4–5; 13.10). It is made clear in this text that angels do not eat (4.9–10); this was also a matter of some dispute (see e.g. *b. Yoma* 4b), with the opposite position being taken in, for example, *Joseph and Aseneth* (*Jos. Asen.* 15.14–15; 16.15; see above, Chapter 3).

Some movement of exegetical traditions between Job and Abraham is in evidence here, as was the case also in the *Testament of Job*. So Abraham, like Job, is celebrated for his hospitality (1.2; cf. 2.2; 4.6; 17.7; cf. Gen. 18.1–8), and the two are explicitly compared at 15.15. The opening conversation in heaven between God and an angel about Abraham also parallels the beginning of the biblical book of Job (1.1–5; 4.6; cf. Job 1.6–12; 2.1–6). The idea that Abraham enjoyed a heavenly vision is found elsewhere in the literature of the Second Temple period (see *L.A.B.* 18.5), but it may also indicate influence from later interpretation of Moses, because some rabbinic sources (see especially *Petirat Moshe* 1.125–8; 6.76–7; *Deuteronomy Rabbah* 11.5, 10) present Moses as protesting about dying before entering the promised land and therefore being granted a heavenly vision.

If this text is indeed a Jewish writing from the first century CE, it attests to a particularly open and universalistic outlook among some Diaspora Jews. Not only are there no references to specifically Jewish laws, and no condemnation of idolatry and gentile immorality, but no clear distinction is drawn between Jew and gentile, since all people alike will be judged on the basis of their deeds. Two interesting details in the narrative in particular serve to illustrate this point. First, the enthroned heavenly judge is identified not with a patriarch or another renowned Jewish figure but with Abel, the son of Adam who was regarded as the father of all humanity: 'For every person is sprung from the first-formed, and on account of this they are judged here by his son' (13.5). Second, when the blessings of the covenant are mentioned, twice, they are interpreted as referring to Abraham's personal wealth and many possessions rather than to his descendants or the land of Israel: 'For I have blessed him as the stars of heaven and as the sand by the seashore, and he lives in abundance, (having) a very large livelihood and many possessions, and he is very rich' (1.5; cf. 4.11; cf. Gen. 22.17). This reading lessens the nationalistic or particularistic effect of one of the scriptural texts most often used to buttress Jewish claims to a unique identity as God's covenant people.

Other examples of testamentary literature

There are no further clear examples of whole works of the testament genre to be found in the Jewish literature of the Second Temple period, although several other writings do include testamentary sections, in which a significant speech is set in the context of a deathbed scene. Abraham is presented as gathering his family together to hear his final words in *Jubilees*, for example (*Jub.* 20.1—21.26), there are mini-testaments in Tobit (Tobit 4.3–21; 14.3–11), 1 Maccabees (1 Macc. 2.49–70) and the *Biblical Antiquities* (see e.g. *L.A.B.* 19.2–5; 24.1–6; 33.1–6), while sections of *1* and *2 Enoch* are also framed as an account of Enoch's departing wisdom and instructions to his descendants (see e.g. *1 En.* 91–105; *2 En.* 14–18). The genre did continue to be popular in Christian circles, however, as is evident in the development and reception of the texts discussed in this chapter. Second-century Christian authors also produced both a *Testament of Isaac* and a *Testament of Jacob*, which appear to derive from the *Testament of Abraham*, and describe the patriarch's death and a heavenly journey. A further early Christian work, the *Testament of Solomon*, which may incorporate older Jewish material, builds on the traditional link between Solomon and exorcism (see e.g. Josephus, *Ant.* 8.44–9) and provides a handbook of demonology and magical healing.

The significance of testaments

The texts discussed in this chapter make use of a common narrative framework, to a greater or lesser extent, but they creatively employ this testamentary form for a variety of purposes and contexts. One, the *Testaments of the Twelve Patriarchs*, provides a moral guide to living a good life; another, the *Testament of Moses*, reassures its readers in difficult times of a glorious future; while both the *Testament of Job* and the *Testament of Abraham* can be read as enjoyable stories in their own right, with a plot line, developed characterization and sense of humour which give them an enduring literary appeal.

The first significant point to note about the testaments is that they highlight particularly clearly the difficulty of drawing any hard and fast distinctions between 'Judaism' and 'Christianity' in the first two or three centuries of the Common Era. It continues to prove problematic, for example, to definitely attribute the *Testaments of the Twelve Patriarchs* or the *Testament of Job* to either Christian or Jewish authorship, or to decide on the extent to which they incorporate older Jewish material. These writings should be taken seriously, therefore, as important evidence for the history and theology of both early Judaism, which produced the Scriptures and exegetical traditions on which they depend, and early Christianity, whose adherents copied, transmitted and read them. They are ancient witnesses to a long process of Christian engagement with the Jewish biblical and exegetical heritage, and even, perhaps, in the case of the *Testaments of the Twelve Patriarchs*, ongoing Christian concern about the ultimate place of Israel in God's plan of salvation for humanity. Reflection on this early tradition of positive interaction might act as a spur to interfaith dialogue and the forging of strong relationships between Jews and Christians today.

The testamentary literature also provides further evidence of the diversity of belief and practice found within late Second Temple Judaism, with the authors of the *Testament of the Twelve Patriarchs* highly valuing the Enochic literature as well as the book of Genesis, for instance, the *Testament of Job* demonstrating an interest in glossolalia and the possibility of mystical communication with angels, and the *Testament of Abraham* demonstrating a remarkably open and tolerant attitude to the universality of judgement and the common humanity of Jews and gentiles. The fact that another of these writings, the *Testament of Moses*, composed in conflict-torn Palestine, stresses, on the other hand, Israel's unique and everlasting covenant relationship with God, and its future glory and exaltation over other nations, illustrates the part which social, historical and geographical context always plays in the shaping of theology.

Second, like all the Jewish texts included in this volume, the testaments provide significant information about the ways in which Scripture was interpreted at this time. Some of the specific exegetical motifs and genres in evidence here, for instance, help to situate within a broader cultural and interpretative context New Testament passages like the Johannine farewell discourses, the call to love one's enemies in the Sermon on the Mount, or the discussion in Luke's Gospel (9.51–56) about calling down fire on those who fail to welcome Jesus.

As with other literary forms, this genre allows for both the provision of answers to questions raised by the biblical narratives, and a greater focus on minor characters, who can act as vehicles for the expression of a contemporary message. In the *Testament of Job*, for instance, his daughters become illustrations of the key theme that the heavenly world is of far greater and more enduring value than the things of this earth, and Joseph's brothers are similarly developed into exemplars of various virtues and vices in the *Testaments of the Twelve Patriarchs*. The freedom which these authors apparently felt to reinterpret even major scriptural figures is striking, however, with rather idealized pictures painted of Job, Moses and Joseph, while Abraham is transformed into a virtual parody of the righteous and obedient patriarch of Genesis. This ability to combine fidelity to the authority of traditional texts with great flexibility in interpreting them is also seen in the works of rewritten Bible, discussed above in Chapter 2. It prompts readers of the Scriptures today to consider for themselves how to achieve the right balance between strict adherence to their words and the creation of meaning from them for a new generation.

Third, some of the theological statements contained within the testaments are also important and worthy of further reflection. These works deal with issues of continued relevance, especially the reality of suffering, the inevitability of death, and the fear which many people experience at the prospect of dying. Thus the consoling teaching that compassion is at the heart of God which shines through the *Testament of Abraham*, with its emphasis on God's mercy and the possibility of repentance, is, for example, one on which believers today may wish to draw.

The development of themes like the effectiveness of intercession is another interesting feature of these texts, evident in the *Testament of Moses*, the *Testament of Abraham* and the *Testaments of the Twelve Patriarchs*, and the former also introduces the distinctive idea that God deliberately 'hardened the hearts' of Israel's enemies. One of the most important theological motifs considered in this chapter is perhaps the implication of the *Testament of Moses* 9.1–7 that the voluntary suffering of the righteous may play some role in bringing about salvation for God's people, especially as similar views seem to have influenced the New Testament understanding of Jesus' death. This passage also serves as a useful reminder that, alongside calls to armed rebellion in the face of foreign invasion or oppression, a pacifist strand existed in Second Temple Judaism, which has continued to inspire both Jews and Christians.

Finally, the testaments also offer significant evidence for the diversity of messianic expectation which characterized early Judaism, from the intriguing figure of Taxo who appears in the *Testament of Moses* through to the variety of saving figures related to Levi and Judah mentioned in the *Testaments of the Twelve Patriarchs*. This issue will emerge also in the discussion of the apocalyptic writings in the next chapter.

Further reading

Allison, D. C., *Testament of Abraham*. 2003, Berlin: de Gruyter

Collins, J. J., *Between Athens and Jerusalem: Jewish Identity in the Hellenistic Diaspora*. 2nd edn. 2000, Grand Rapids, Michigan/Cambridge: Eerdmans

Davila, J. R., *The Provenance of the Pseudepigrapha: Jewish, Christian or Other?* 2005, Leiden: Brill

Haralambakis, M., *The Testament of Job: Text, Narrative and Reception History*. 2012, London: T&T Clark

Kugler, R. A., *The Testaments of the Twelve Patriarchs*. 2001, Sheffield: Sheffield Academic Press

Ludlow, J. W., *Abraham Meets Death: Narrative Humour in the Testament of Abraham*. 2002, London: Sheffield Academic Press

Nickelsburg, G. W. E., *Jewish Literature between the Bible and the Mishnah*. 2nd edn. 2005, Minneapolis: Fortress Press

6

Apocalyptic literature

Introducing the genre of apocalyptic literature

Apocalyptic is perhaps the best known of all the genres discussed in this volume, and it forms a substantial and significant component of the literary output of the Second Temple period. The term 'apocalypse' comes from a Greek word meaning 'revelation' or 'unveiling', and considerable effort has been devoted by modern commentators like John Collins to the task of defining the form and nature of this literature more fully and precisely.[1] It is generally accepted that a distinction should be drawn between the literary genre 'apocalypse' and the apocalyptic world-view or 'apocalypticism', which can be present in texts which are not formally apocalypses. The simplest definition of the form is that an apocalypse is a collection of revelatory visions held together by a narrative framework. This revelation is always attributed to a revered figure from Israel's past, such as Daniel or Enoch, and its authoritative status rests on the claim that the seer has received and now transmits to others heavenly revelation which is not generally available. This information is usually disclosed to him by an interpreting angel or other supernatural being, not by God directly. There are two main types of apocalypse, one containing a heavenly journey and the other a review of history, and these can be combined within one larger work, as in the case of *1 Enoch*.

Apocalypticism as a belief system is characterized by the view that this world is disordered, so there is a need for a divine intervention to restore it to its intended state. This will involve a final judgement, expected imminently, in which sinners will be punished and the righteous rewarded. The apocalyptic perspective is dualistic, dividing humanity into two definite camps, the good and the bad, and envisaging the clear-cut separation of this present age from the world to

---

[1] See e.g. J. J. Collins, *The Apocalyptic Imagination: An Introduction to Jewish Apocalyptic Literature.* 2nd edn. 1998, Grand Rapids, Michigan/Cambridge, UK: Eerdmans.

come. It is also deterministic, arguing that when history is viewed as a whole, from its beginning to its inevitable end, it demonstrates that God is firmly in control of all events, despite any appearances to the contrary, and has decided their outcome in advance. Apocalyptic literature may be particularly renowned for its eschatological teaching, or future expectations, but it also contains extensive discussion of many other kinds of knowledge, including botany, geography, cosmology, astronomy and angelology. One of the most pressing questions with which it attempts to deal is how to explain the presence of sin and evil in a world supposedly created by a good God.

The origins of the apocalyptic genre have traditionally been linked with marginalized and oppressed groups, because of its focus on a reversal of the current world order, and also its use of symbols, which might be assumed to have functioned as a sort of code, intelligible only to a small, persecuted group. More recently, this theory has been discounted and replaced with a growing recognition that the early Jewish apocalypses are far more likely to have been produced within learned, elite circles, by people who had the time, means and education necessary to engage in the required serious study of the Scriptures and other traditions, and perhaps also to travel widely to acquire further knowledge.[2] Apocalyptic writings show the influence of both the prophetic and wisdom traditions. So, like the wisdom literature, apocalypses reflect an interest in nature and learning, and there are some shared perspectives, such as the distinction between the wise and the foolish, and the acceptance that the course of history is predetermined. Meanwhile, the prophetic corpus provides the model for the very concept of divine communication with human beings, for apocalyptic visions of God's throne and for the use of symbolism. It is important to realize, however, that although some of the imagery found in these apocalyptic texts might appear bizarre to modern readers, it was employed with the very practical purpose of dealing with live and important issues, such as the presence of violence and inequality in society, or the experience of despair among communities suffering from economic hardships, conflict or poor governance.

---

[2] The earlier view has been challenged by, for example, Stephen Cook; see his *Prophecy and Apocalypticism: The Postexilic Social Setting.* 1995, Minneapolis: Fortress Press.

1 Enoch

Introduction to *1 Enoch*

The *Book of Enoch* or *1 Enoch* is a collection of writings spanning at least three centuries, which are all associated with the biblical figure of that name, the great-grandfather of Noah (Gen. 5.18–24). Enoch is presented as a wise and righteous scribe (e.g. 12.4; 15.1; cf. 74.2; 81.6) and visionary, who is given access to heavenly secrets and knowledge of the future. The authority of his revelations is guaranteed by their ancient setting, in the era before the flood. Very little information is given about Enoch in the Scriptures, but one cryptic statement provides a key to much of the later interpretation of him: 'Enoch walked with God; and he was not, for God took him' (Gen. 5.24). This was generally read as an indication of his exceptional virtue, and the unusual reference to his passing prompted speculation that he did not die, but rather ascended into heaven. His reported age at death of 365 years (Gen. 5.23), the exact number of days in a solar year and a remarkably short life-span for a patriarch, may also be a factor in his subsequent association with astrological and calendrical knowledge. Jewish thinking about Enoch also seems to have been influenced by Ancient Near Eastern mythology. The hero of the Mesopotamian flood narrative, Atrahasis or Utnapishtim, for instance, was thought to have been shown the secret of the impending deluge by the gods (cf. *1 En.* 83.2–5), and connections may have been drawn between Enoch, the seventh generation from Adam, and the famous seventh Sumerian king Enmeduranki.

Parts of *1 Enoch* were composed before the later scriptural writings and comprise some of the oldest extant examples of apocalyptic writing. This literature provides, therefore, extremely important information about the evolution of the apocalyptic genre as a whole, as well as about the historical development of the Enochic tradition. The following five major books, of varying lengths, can be identified:

- the Book of the Watchers (chapters 1—36), from the third century BCE;
- the Similitudes of Enoch or the Parables of Enoch (chapters 37—71), from the late first century BCE or early first century CE;

127

- the Astronomical Book or the Book of the Luminaries (chapters 72—82), from the third century BCE;
- the Book of Dreams (chapters 83—90), from the second century BCE, which includes the significant independent unit called the Animal Apocalypse (chapters 85—90);
- the Epistle of Enoch (chapters 91—108), from the second century BCE, which includes the Apocalypse of Weeks (93.1–10; 91.11–17).

A similar fivefold division is found in other Jewish writings, including the Pentateuch, the book of Psalms and the *Pirke Aboth*, a compilation of rabbinic ethical teaching.[3] Although the various sections of *1 Enoch* were originally composed separately, they clearly engage with the same literary and theological tradition, and share a recognizable and distinct world-view.

Evidence about the communities who produced this Enochic corpus is, unfortunately, scarce, but their output was clearly valued at Qumran, and is also reflected in several other writings discussed in this volume, such as *Jubilees* (see above, Chapter 2) and the *Testaments of the Twelve Patriarchs* (see above, Chapter 5). They are linked by some commentators to the early stages of the Essene movement, or to the group of the *hasidim* or 'pious ones' who were reportedly active at the time of the Maccabean Revolt (1 Macc. 2.42; 7.13; 2 Macc. 14.6).[4] Since *1 Enoch* places noticeably little emphasis on the theme of the covenant or on the Mosaic law, it has been suggested that it represents a different form of Judaism from that which became mainstream in the rabbinic era after the fall of Jerusalem. However, while this focus on the figure of Enoch rather than Moses certainly attests to the breadth of Second Temple Judaism, it does result at least partly from the text's narrative setting in the pre-flood era, well before the events of Sinai.

1 Enoch has survived primarily in Ethiopic, but some sections are also extant in Greek, the language from which the Ethiopic translation was made in the fifth or sixth century CE. Following a significant

---

[3] It is unlikely, therefore, that this arrangement signals that *1 Enoch* was deliberately presented as an alternative to the Mosaic Pentateuch as has been proposed by, for example, Jozef Milik; see his *The Books of Enoch: Aramaic Fragments of Qumran Cave 4*. 1976, Oxford: Clarendon Press.
[4] This view is particularly associated with Gabriele Boccaccini; see e.g. G. Boccaccini, J. H. Ellens and J. A. Waddell (eds), *Enoch and Qumran Origins: New Light on a Forgotten Connection*. 2005, Grand Rapids, Michigan: Eerdmans.

discovery at Qumran, 11 manuscripts containing fragments in the original Aramaic of all parts of the work except the latest section, the Similitudes, are now available. *1 Enoch* was almost certainly composed in Palestine, and is one of the most important of the extant writings of the Second Temple period, because of its length, its theological content, its relationship to crucial periods of Jewish history such as the reign of Antiochus IV Epiphanes and the Maccabean Revolt, and its ongoing influence on both Judaism and Christianity. The Enochic tradition is preserved and developed in the later works *2 Enoch* and *3 Enoch*, quoted in the New Testament (Jude 14–15), and frequently referred to in the writings of the early church fathers, such as Origen and Tertullian. It is still included in the canon of Scripture in the Ethiopian Orthodox Church and is also highly regarded by the Church of the Latter-Day Saints.

Key features of *1 Enoch*

The main characteristic features of the apocalyptic genre can all be found in *1 Enoch*, including revelatory visions, heavenly journeys, interpreting angels and historical reviews. Influence from both the wisdom and the prophetic tradition is in evidence throughout. Like many of the biblical prophets, for instance, Enoch is pictured as experiencing a call, a throne-vision and other forms of divine communication. Allusions to the prophetic literature are widespread, with especially frequent allusion to the description of the renewal of Creation in Trito-Isaiah (Isa. 65.8—66.16; cf. e.g. *1 En.* 5.5–10; 10.16–22; 25.5–6; 90.28–38; 91.13–16) and to Daniel's vision of the Ancient of Days (Dan. 7.9–14; cf. e.g. *1 En.* 46.1–7; 48.1–10). Enoch is also, however, specifically called a scribe (e.g. 12.1), and his revelation is termed 'a vision of wisdom' (37.1).[5] He engages in the observation of nature characteristic of the wise person (e.g. 2.1—3.1), and the idea that humanity falls into two groups, the foolish and the wise, is pervasive (see e.g. 98.9—99.10; 104.9—105.2; cf. 32.1–5; 92.1; 94.1–5). A range of other literary genres is also employed, including prayers (e.g. 84.2–4) and woes (see e.g. chapters 94—99). In addition, parts of the work read like a testament, with the Epistle of Enoch

---

[5] All translations of the text are taken from G. W. E. Nickelsburg and J. C. Vanderkam, *1 Enoch: A New Translation*. 2004, Minneapolis: Fortress Press.

in particular introduced as his last words to his descendants (see 91.1–3).

Important themes in *1 Enoch*

The different sections of *1 Enoch* reflect a variety of theological emphases, and each of them will be considered in turn below in order to highlight more fully some of the most significant aspects of each book. Developments within the tradition can clearly be seen, in the attitude to the Temple, for example, or in the explanations offered for the presence of sin in the world. Nevertheless, a shared perspective and a range of common themes are present across the whole text, and the various authors are consciously interacting with one another. Fundamental to their world-view is the conviction that the present world is full of wickedness and injustice, and the consequent hope for an impending divine intervention to eradicate this evil and renew Creation.

The expectation that God will soon come in judgement is expressed from the first chapter of *1 Enoch* to the last, although no one systematic picture is given of this event. This theme of judgement is presented as a positive rather than a fearful message, as it is intended to console those who may be enduring suffering and oppression with the belief that something better awaits them. The scriptural flood narrative is a paradigm for this future act of God, so the figure of Noah is prominent throughout *1 Enoch*, and pre-existing sources about him may have been incorporated (see e.g. 10.1–22; 54.7–55.2; 60.1–25; 65.1—67.3; 106.1–19).

As noted above, the importance of Moses and the Sinai covenant may be downplayed in this tradition. The giving of the law is omitted from the extensive review of history in the Animal Apocalypse, for example, although it is referred to positively in the Apocalypse of Weeks (93.6), and it is Enoch, not Moses, who experiences theophanies (e.g. 14.8–25; 39.2–14; 46.1–2; 71.1–17), blesses the people (see especially 1.1) and intercedes on behalf of others, even fallen angels (e.g. 13.4). The commandments lie in the background of some of the text's ethical teaching, for example: 'But you have not stood firm nor acted according to his commandments' (5.4). However, the moral instruction in *1 Enoch* is generally closer to the form characteristic of the wisdom literature rather than the Pentateuch, appealing to the general laws of nature, for instance, and drawing comparisons between the order of Creation and human reluctance to follow God's ways (e.g. 5.1–4; 101.1–9).

The Enochic authors understood God as a totally transcendent being, as evidenced by the titles applied to him, such as 'Holy One' and 'God of Glory', and also by the profound awe which the throne-visions inspire in Enoch (e.g. 14.8–25). This supreme being does not administer the created world directly, but through a host of angels: 'I saw thousands of thousands and ten thousand times ten thousand – they were innumerable and incalculable – who were standing before the glory of the Lord of Spirits' (40.1; cf. 20.1–7; 40.1–10; 69.1–14). Their names and precise roles are disclosed to the seer as part of the esoteric knowledge to which he is made privy (e.g. 20.1–7; 40.1–10).

The Book of the Watchers

The first book of *1 Enoch* sets the scene for the whole work, and introduces many of the themes which will recur in later sections, especially the prospect of God's imminent judgement, which is the main focus of chapters 1—16. The reason for the presence of evil in the world is also a major theme here, and the origins of sin are not attributed, as in some traditions, to the disobedience of Adam (Gen. 3.1–24; cf. *4 Ezra* 3.20–6; 4.30; 7.118; *2 Bar.* 23.4; 48.42–3; 54.15; 56.5–8), but to an angelic rebellion against God. The story of the coming to earth of heavenly beings who mate with human women, known also from Genesis 6.1–4, is therefore told here in a much more elaborate form (6.1—10.22). It is these fallen angels who are said to have led human beings astray, by teaching them all kinds of things which God did not intend them to know, such as how to make weapons of war, and how to ornament them-selves with make-up and jewellery (8.1–2). Even when God intervenes to remove these disobedient angels and bind them in the depths of the earth until the day of judgement (10.4–6, 11–15), demons emerge from their bodies (15.9–12), so wickedness remains on the earth. These angels are sometimes called 'watchers', a term which gives this section of *1 Enoch* its name, and which probably indicates that they were understood to function either as guardians of the heavens or surveyors of the earth. This narrative assumes a very significant place within the Enochic tradition (see also e.g. 64.1–2; 69.1–15; 86.1–6), and it affirms the supernatural rather than human origins of sin, although individual responsibility for sin is affirmed elsewhere in the text (e.g. 98.4), perhaps indicating some theological development over time. There is no focus anywhere in *1 Enoch* on Adam's sin, however; so, for example, even in the review of Israel's history in the Animal Apocalypse, the first wicked act referred to is Cain's murder of Abel (85.4; cf. 22.6–7).

In the second part of the Book of the Watchers (chapters 17—36), Enoch is taken on a heavenly tour, a motif which reassures the audience that the revelation he is passing on to them is authoritative and trustworthy. It is possible that the author really had travelled widely, and a learned tradition of cosmological speculation is certainly in evidence in these chapters (cf. e.g. 41.3–7; 72.1—79.6). He is also granted a vision of God's heavenly throne (14.8–25), which echoes several scriptural passages, especially those which describe the commissioning of the prophets (e.g. 1 Kings 22.19; Isa. 6.1–4; Ezek. 1.3–28; Hab. 3.3–15; cf. Dan. 7.9–14). The awesome nature of this experience and the utter transcendence of God is underlined, with the seer presented as trembling and unable to either look at God (14.20–4) or adequately describe God's house, which is, for example, both 'hot as fire and cold as snow' (14.13). This theme of mystical ascent to heaven is a very important aspect of apocalyptic literature, and is further developed in the later *merkavah* tradition. It possibly reflects a view that the official cult was not functioning effectively, so that alternative forms of divine access were needed.

The language of the 'elect' and 'righteous' is frequently applied to Enoch's community, beginning with the very first verse of the text, and its members are frequently distinguished from the 'sinners' or the wicked (e.g. 1.1; 5.5–10; cf. 38.1–6; 45.1–6; 94.1—103.18). They can be confident that they will be rewarded in the coming judgement with peace, plenty and happiness (e.g. 1.7–8; 5.7, 10; 10.18—11.2; cf. *2 Bar.* 29.5). The hope is expressed also that at this time all of Israel will become righteous and the gentiles will turn to worship of Israel's God (10.21; cf. 48.4). The descriptions of this anticipated glorious future echo the scriptural creation accounts, and a definite correspondence emerges throughout *1 Enoch* between the end times and the beginning of the world. One scene, for example, envisages the planting of a fragrant tree to provide life-giving fruit for the righteous, recalling the tree at the centre of the Garden of Eden, from which the first humans were prohibited from eating (25.4–5; cf. 90.37; cf. Gen. 2.15–17; 3.2–6). Salvation will be realized in a renewed earth (10.18—11.2), a picture which provides an important counter-balance to forms of future expectation which focus exclusively on the heavenly world, since it recognizes the essential goodness of God's Creation, and can encourage a heightened concern for the environment, or a greater political engagement to help bring about a transformation of the earth.

Similitudes of Enoch

This book is the latest part of *1 Enoch*, and the fact that no trace of it has been discovered at Qumran has contributed to suggestions that it should be dated to the late first century CE and may even be a Christian composition. The current scholarly consensus, how-ever, is that it was composed in, or shortly after, the reign of Herod the Great (37–4 BCE), and is a Jewish composition, since it makes no reference to Jesus or to any specifically Christian themes. It is made up of three subsections or 'parables' (chapters 38—44; 45—57; 58—69), each including a description of a judgement scene. Its main themes, then, echo those already identified in the Book of the Watchers: divine judgement and the future salvation of the com-munity of the righteous and elect ones.

The imagery and language of this section is heavily influenced by the report of the vision of the divine throne in Daniel 7.9–14. Echoes of this passage are especially clear in the introduction of a 'son of man' (e.g. 46.3–4; 48.2; 62.7; 63.11; 70.1; 71.14, 17), who is pres-ently hidden in heaven but who will be revealed at the end of time. He is associated above all with righteousness (e.g. 46.3), and he will be involved in the enacting of God's punishment on the wicked: 'And this son of man whom you have seen . . . He will loosen the reins of the strong, and he will crush the teeth of the sinners. He will overturn the kings from their thrones and their kingdoms' (46.4–5). Various other titles are applied in the Similitudes to this redeemer, including the righteous one, the chosen one, and the anointed one or Messiah, and he is also reminiscent of the servant of Deutero-Isaiah, since: 'he will be the light of the nations, and he will be a hope for those who grieve in their hearts' (48.4; cf. Isa. 42.6–7). A variety of messianic expectations are combined here in one figure, then, although, interestingly, there is no mention of his having Davidic lineage. He seems to be the heavenly counterpart of the earthly community of the righteous or chosen ones. They are enduring suffering and perhaps even persecution on earth (see e.g. 47.1; 48.7; 53.7; 62.11), but will be vindicated in the coming judgement and will then share in his exaltation (e.g. 41.2; 45.5–6).

In its use of the phrase 'son of man', the Similitudes may represent an early Jewish stage in the development of what was originally a non-specific figure of speech meaning simply 'human being' into a distinct messianic title. It may, therefore, provide a significant parallel for the application of this term to Jesus in the New Testament Gospels, and it is possible that the author of Matthew in particular was influenced by the Similitudes or a similar source in his presentation of Jesus as a son of man and heavenly judge (see e.g. Matt. 25.31–46). This book certainly affords important evidence for the diversity of early Jewish messianic expectation (cf. *4 Ezra*). It also opens up the question of whether belief in a second divine figure could be entertained in Second Temple Judaism. At the very end of the book, Enoch is himself identified with this heavenly son of man (71.14). This chapter is possibly a late addition, and some commentators see it as a deliberate attempt to provide a Jewish alternative to contemporary Christian claims about Jesus.

Another distinctive feature of this book is the frequent use of the title 'Lord of the Spirits' for God. This name is not used in the other sections of *1 Enoch*, but does fit with the general picture of God as always surrounded by myriads of angels, and is probably a development of the scriptural designation 'Lord of Hosts'. The Similitudes are also noteworthy for the trenchant criticism which they express towards rulers, landlords, the wealthy and the powerful (e.g. 62.1— 63.12; 94.7–8; 96.4–8; 97.8–10; 102.9). A commitment to social justice is an important strand within apocalyptic writing (cf. the *Sibylline Oracles*, see above, Chapter 4), since these authors hope for the complete reversal of earthly power structures in the world to come. A further interesting point made in this section is that wisdom can only be found in heaven and not on earth (42.1–2). Since the very opposite view is expressed in Sirach (Sir. 24.7–11, 23), this may be a direct challenge to some contemporary wisdom schools, and perhaps above all to the belief that wisdom is to be solely and completely identified with the Torah, which would have allowed no place for the additional Enochic revelatory traditions.

The Astronomical Book

This section is a kind of compendium of ancient knowledge about astronomy and cosmology, which serves to illustrate the association of apocalyptic literature with learned circles. The Aramaic form of this book found at Qumran is considerably longer than the extant Ethiopic version. Its main theological significance lies in its discussion of the length of the year, where it is argued that a solar year lasts for 364 days, not 360 as some apparently maintained (e.g. 82.6). This may indicate a connection between *1 Enoch* and the wider debate within Second Temple Judaism about the correct calendrical system, reflected in *Jubilees* (see Chapter 2, above) and some of the Qumran texts. This is not necessarily the case, however, since there does not seem to be any opposition expressed here to a 354-day lunar calendar, nor any emphasis on the need to date festivals properly.

Book of Dreams

The two dream-visions which have been put together in this section were originally composed as independent units. Enoch first describes a vision of the flood which he claims to have experienced early in his life (83.2). This account is followed by the Animal Apocalypse (chapters 85—90), which, like the book of Daniel, was produced during the time of the unpopular emperor Antiochus IV Epiphanes (175–164 BCE) and the Maccabean Revolt (167–164 BCE).

This is a very significant early apocalypse, which reviews history from the time of the creation, using symbols and colours to denote various people and nations. Human beings are represented by animals, so that righteous characters like Adam and Noah are depicted as white bulls (85.3; 89.1), for example, and the Egyptians as wolves (89.13–27). Angels are equated with human beings (e.g. 87.2) or stars (e.g. 86.3), and Israel's negligent leaders are called shepherds (89.59—90.25; cf. Ezek. 34.1–16). The greatest amount of space and detail, approximately one sixth of the whole, is devoted to the time before the flood (85.3—89.8). This author's support for the Maccabean cause is clear from the description of Judas Maccabeus as a horned sheep successfully battling, with God's help, against Israel's enemies, who are portrayed as predatory ravens (90.9–16).

The review ends, as expected, with a judgement scene, in which the wrongs inflicted on righteous Israelites by violent gentile nations will be avenged and the wicked destroyed (90.17–38). Then the renewal of Creation is envisaged, when the earth will return to the state of peace and righteousness which God originally intended for it (90.33), and a new Jerusalem will be erected on earth, a far bigger and more beautiful place than formerly (90.28–9; cf. Isa. 65.17–25). Interestingly, this passage does not specifically state that a new temple will be built in the restored city, and dissatisfaction with the Second Temple is expressed earlier in the vision: 'And they began to place a table before the tower, but all the bread on it was polluted and not pure' (89.73). This omission may imply that the author and his community were not looking for the re-establishment of the Temple (cf. Rev. 21.22), although such a hope is expressed in the Apocalypse of Weeks (93.13), which may illustrate some internal development within the Enochic tradition. The birth of a snow-white cow at this time is also predicted (90.37). This animal is generally understood as a symbol for the Messiah, and he corresponds to the first pure white creature to emerge from the earth, Adam (85.3), echoing the message of the Book of the Watchers that the eschaton will parallel the time of the original creation (e.g. 25.4–5). No messianic functions are attributed to him, however, such as judging or ruling, and he appears only after God has brought about salvation for the righteous. This vision is unusual in not being followed by an interpretation, which may indicate that it was easily intelligible to its original audience.

Epistle of Enoch

The most significant unit within the Epistle of Enoch is the Apocalypse of Weeks. The order of this section has been disturbed in the Ethiopic version, but in the Aramaic fragments found at Qumran, 93.3–14 is placed before 91.12–17, which makes better sense. It provides a review of history divided into predetermined periods (cf. 92.2), with some correspondences to the longer Animal Apocalypse. History is divided into ten periods, called 'weeks', some of which are considered to have been good, such as the age of Abraham in the third week, but others, like the second week containing the flood, are depicted as evil. The seventh epoch runs from the Babylonian exile to the author's own time in the era of the Hellenizing emperor Antiochus IV Epiphanes (93.9–14). This marks the turning point of history, since it will be followed by future judgement and the extension of God's reign over the whole earth for ever (91.14–17).

Apart from this apocalyptic section, the Epistle of Enoch contains extensive ethical exhortation, with a pronounced focus on the theme of social justice, similar to that found elsewhere in *1 Enoch*, especially in the Similitudes:

> Woe to you who acquire gold and silver unjustly and say, 'We have become very wealthy, and we have gotten possessions, and we have acquired all that we wished . . .' You err! For your wealth will not remain, but will quickly ascend from you; for you have acquired everything unjustly, and you will be delivered to a great curse . . .
>
> (97.8–10; cf. 46.4–7; 62.2–6; 94.7–8; 96.4–8; 102.9)

4 Ezra

Introduction to *4 Ezra*

4 Ezra offers a theological response to the destruction of Jerusalem by Roman forces in 70 CE. A religious leader and visionary called Ezra is portrayed as wrestling with deep questions about divine justice and God's relationship to the people of Israel in the aftermath of this disaster. Through a series of heavenly revelations he is empowered to move beyond his initial feelings of anguish and even anger at God to a point where he is able to offer comfort and hope to his community in their distress.

The text was almost certainly composed in Hebrew, then translated into Greek at an early stage, but it is extant only in later versions including Latin, Syriac, Ethiopic, Armenian, Arabic and Georgian. It was preserved and transmitted in early Christian circles, and a new framework created for it. The original Jewish apocalypse now forms chapters 3—14 of an expanded Christian work, therefore, known by the title 2 Esdras, which is traditionally included in the collection of the Apocrypha, but is not one of the deutero-canonical books accepted as scriptural by the Roman Catholic Church. Later Christian writings, such as the *Apocalypse of Esdras* and the *Apocalypse of Sedrach* draw on *4 Ezra*/2 Esdras, and the work remained popular throughout the mediaeval and early modern periods, inspiring, for example, both Christopher Columbus and John Milton.

The narrative is ostensibly set among the Judaean exiles in Babylon in the sixth century BCE, 'in the thirtieth year after the destruction of our city' (3.1; cf. 3.28; 4.28–9; 10.20–3).[6] This is, however, a cryptic reference to the second fall of Jerusalem, with 'Babylon' functioning as a code for 'Rome'. The figure of 30 years after the destruction is an approximate rather than an exact indication of the time of composition, as it echoes the traditional date for the beginning of the ministry of the prophet Ezekiel (Ezek. 1.1). The late first-century CE context of the text is confirmed by one of the vision reports, which describes the appearance of a multi-headed eagle (11.1–35), symbolizing the Roman Empire. Its three heads (11.1) are usually understood as denoting the Flavian emperors, Vespasian, Titus and Domitian, who ruled from 69 to 96 CE.[7]

The narrator's pseudonym is Ezra, after the scribe who, according to Scripture, played a central role in restoring observance of the Mosaic law among the returned exiles in the fifth century BCE. However, he introduces himself initially as 'Salathiel who is also called Ezra' (3.1). Salathiel or Shealtiel is the name of the father of Zerubbabel, who is associated with the return of the first group of Judaeans from Babylon and the rebuilding of the Temple. This dual identification may be an attempt to resolve the chronological difficulty of attributing a work set in the immediate aftermath of the first destruction of Jerusalem to Ezra, who was not actually active until more than a century later. It may also serve to link Ezra with another apocalyptic seer who was given two names, Daniel and Belteshazzar (Dan. 4.8), and it is a particularly fitting designation for a character who will

---

[6] All quotations of the text are taken from M. E. Stone, *Fourth Ezra: A Commentary on the Book of Fourth Ezra.* 1990, Minneapolis: Fortress Press.

[7] That is the view of the majority of commentators, although some have argued that the later Roman emperor Severus and his two sons, Geta and Caracalla (193–217 CE), are in view. If that is the case, the original account of the vision was perhaps updated in the early third century, since *4 Ezra* as a whole clearly reflects a time soon after the destruction of Jerusalem in 70 CE. See e.g. L. DiTommaso, 'Dating the Eagle Vision of *4 Ezra*: A New Look at an Old Theory'. *JSP* (1999), pp. 3–38.

be portrayed as passionately interrogating God, since in Hebrew it means 'I have asked God'. Nothing is known about the real author of the apocalypse, and although the narrator is presented as a leader of his community (5.16; 12.40), this may simply be part of the narrative fiction that he is the new Ezra for the people of his time. He situates himself in Babylon (3.1), which may indicate that he was writing in Rome. However, most commentators do not interpret this verse literally, regarding it as more likely that the work was composed in Israel, and that its central concern was to encourage Jews left in the land to deal with life after their crushing defeat.

Key features of *4 Ezra*

4 Ezra is made up of seven sections, each containing either a dialogue between the seer and an angel named Uriel or a vision and its interpretation. This structure may reflect the traditional understanding of seven as a perfect number. The text illustrates several features characteristic of the apocalyptic genre, such as an interpreting angel (e.g. 4.1; 5.31–2; 7.1–2; 10.29–40; 12.10–13), lists of signs of the end (5.1–13; 6.20–4; 9.3–6), a historical review (3.4–19) and the division of time into periods (5.5; 6.7; 7.44). Its outlook is often described as pessimistic and deterministic, as there is a clear sense that Creation is already past its best (5.55; cf. 6.20; 14.10–12) and that the kingdoms of this world are drawing towards their inevitable end (11.44; cf. 4.36–7; 7.44, 74). A similar view is expressed in parts of the *Sibylline Oracles* (see above, Chapter 4), and by some Greek authors like Hesiod.

Older material is reused and updated in *4 Ezra*, as in *1 Enoch* and other apocalypses. The clearest example of this comes in the interpretation of the eagle vision:

> The eagle which you saw coming up from the sea is the fourth kingdom which appeared in a vision to your brother Daniel [i.e. Dan. 7.2–18]. But it was not explained to him as I now explain it to you . . .
>
> (12.11–12)

A similar identification of of the fourth beast of Daniel's vision with the Roman Empire is made in other contemporary apocalypses (Rev. 13.1–18; cf. *2 Bar.* 39.5). The account of the apparition of the man from the sea (13.1–13) may also draw on pre-existing sources, as the explanation given (13.21–50) does not exactly match the details of the vision.

4 Ezra is of particular significance for the ongoing debate about the roots of apocalyptic, since it has many features in common with wisdom writings, especially Sirach and the Qumran text *4QInstruction.*[8] Typically wisdom literary forms employed in *4 Ezra* include riddles (4.5–8) and parables (5.13–18), and shared themes also occur, such as an interest in Creation and natural phenomena (4.7; 6.1–4, 38–54), and the idea that the wise person is widely travelled (3.29, 33; cf. Sir. 34.10–11). There are obvious parallels with the book of Job, too, in the lengthy dialogues and challenges to the reality of God's justice.

However, the work is not influenced only by the wisdom tradition, but has links also with prophecy: Ezra is specifically called a prophet (12.42; cf. 7.130); he experiences symbolic visions like some of the scriptural prophets; and, in an incident reminiscent of the calling of figures like Isaiah and Jeremiah, he has a direct encounter with God in which he is given the task of instructing and encouraging the people (14.1–13). This passage connects the seer above all with Moses, Israel's greatest teacher and prophet, since God calls to him from within a bush (14.1–3) and communicates with him for 40 days and nights (14.42–5; cf. *2 Bar.* 76.4). He is then instructed to record these revelations in a set of books, 24 of which are immediately made public, but a further 70, a number symbolizing perfection or completeness, are restricted to the circle of the wise (14.45–7; cf. 14.26). The idea that on Mount Sinai Moses received secret, additional information as well as the Torah is widespread in early Jewish literature (see e.g. *Jub.* 1.4; *L.A.B.* 19.10; *T. Mos.* 1.16–17; *2 Bar.* 59.4–11; *Leviticus Rabbah* 26.4; *Numbers Rabbah* 34.2), and this tradition was used to authenticate apocalyptic teachings. The writings which are available to everyone are generally understood to be those which would form the Hebrew Bible, but these verses provide the earliest extant evidence for the view that there are 24 books which should be accorded scriptural status, although this figure is not actually given in every version of the text.

---

[8] See e.g. D. J. Harrington, 'Wisdom and Apocalyptic in *4QInstruction* and *4 Ezra*'. In *Wisdom and Apocalypticism in the Dead Sea Scrolls and in the Biblical Tradition.* Ed. F. Garcia Martinez. 2003, Leuven: Leuven University Press, pp. 343–55.

The most striking and original element in *4 Ezra* is a series of lengthy conversations between the seer and an angel named Uriel which run throughout the first seven chapters. In them, Ezra asks several deep questions, and often protests that the answers he receives are inadequate or even wrong (see e.g. 4.12, 33, 44, 51; 7.45–8, 106, 116). Intriguingly, it is not immediately obvious which of the speakers in these dialogues is to be taken as articulating the correct theological perspective. It seems most natural, for instance, to assume that the angel is voicing the words of God, but it then becomes difficult to understand why the righteous and revered Ezra is set up as the spokesperson for flawed ways of thinking. These exchanges may represent competing contemporary responses to the recent national catastrophe, with some groups perhaps emphasizing traditional covenantal theology, and others placing their hopes in the in-breaking of a radically different eschatological future. However, it is not possible to simply identify the narrator with one school of thought and the angel with another, since they agree on some issues, and no one view clearly emerges as the right one. By the end of the narrative, for example, Ezra seems to have moved closer to Uriel's position in some respects, yet several of the problems which he raises in the early dialogues remain unresolved. In a recent study, therefore, Karina Hogan has suggested that this indefinite outcome may be a deliberate strategy on the part of the author to show that none of the current explanations for the crisis of faith caused by the destruction of Jerusalem are fully satisfying for the truly wise person, who can ultimately, like Ezra, find consolation only in religious experience and symbols.[9]

Important themes in *4 Ezra*

4 Ezra could be described as a theodicy as well as an apocalypse, as it tackles the problem of how the people with whom God has supposedly made an everlasting covenant could have been so comprehensively defeated by the Romans. The genuine grief of the narrator at the affliction of his people repeatedly shines through:

---

[9] See K. M. Hogan, *Theologies in Conflict in 4 Ezra: Wisdom Debate and Apocalyptic Solution.* 2008, Leiden: Brill.

I was troubled as I lay on my bed, and my thoughts welled up in my heart, because I saw the desolation of Zion and the wealth of those who lived in Babylon. My spirit was greatly agitated, and I began to speak anxious words to the Most High . . .

(3.1–3; cf. 5.21, 34; 6.37; 8.15–16)

Thus Ezra protests that he would rather be an inanimate animal (7.62–9) or not have been born at all (4.12) than have to endure the agony of suffering without understanding the reason for it. In the opening dialogues, therefore, he forcefully questions why the covenant appears to have been broken (3.15; 4.23; 5.29), why God has permitted the destruction of the holy city of Jerusalem, and why the gentiles who inflicted this carnage are not punished but allowed to prosper (3.2; 5.29; 6.56–9).

The angel Uriel replies with the traditional explanations that human beings cannot expect to understand God's ways (4.10–11, 21, 34; 5.34) and that the people of Israel have brought their fate on themselves by choosing to sin and disobey the divine commandments (7.20–4, 72, 127–30; cf. 8.56–60). He also offers the reassurance that any apparent injustices will be resolved in the end times (4.26–7), when the righteous will receive their reward (7.11–14, 88–101, 123; 8.52–4).

These attempts at a justification for the events of 70 CE fail to satisfy Ezra, who is still exercised by two issues in particular. First, he objects that the Israelites are literally unable to keep the law which they were given by God since all people have inherited an evil heart from their common ancestor Adam (3.20–6; 7.48, 68, 118; cf. *2 Bar.* 23.4; 48.42–3; 54.15–19; 56.5–8). Uriel agrees with this negative view of human nature, but is not perturbed by it as Ezra is, simply declaring that the evil sown by Adam's sin must reach its full measure before the end times can be inaugurated: 'for a grain of evil seed was sown in Adam's heart from the beginning, and how much fruit of ungodliness it has produced until now, and will produce until the time of threshing comes' (4.30). The difficulty of reconciling a belief in a general post-fall tendency to sinfulness with human freedom to act righteously is not resolved in the text, but it certainly throws some extremely interesting light on early Christian discussion of the same subject (see e.g. Rom. 5.12–21; 7.4–25).

The seer's second major concern centres on the small number of people who will actually enjoy the promised future paradise (7.46–8, 60–1, 116–26; 8.1–3, 41; 9.14; 10.10). Apparently without regret, Uriel asserts that: 'The Most High made this world for the sake of many, but the world to come for the sake of few' (8.1). Ezra, however, challenges God directly about this: 'If then you will quickly destroy him who with so great labour was fashioned by your command, to what purpose was he made?' (8.14). That this was a live issue in contemporary theological debate is evident from the New Testament Gospels, where the same question is asked: 'Lord, will those who are saved be few?' (Luke 13.23; cf. Matt. 22.14; cf. *2 Bar.* 21.11).

4 Ezra does not, then, follow the *Testament of Abraham* in fore-grounding divine mercy (see above, Chapter 5), although it is clearly stated here that God has an abundance of compassion (7.132–40), loves Creation intensely (8.47; cf. 5.33, 40), and did not make people with the intention of destroying them, but is simply responding to their sinfulness (8.59–60). Thus the readers are assured that: 'there shall not be grief at their destruction, so much as joy over those to whom salvation is assured' (7.131; cf. *T. Ab.* 11.11). No conclusive solution to this second problem of how a good and forgiving God can deprive most human beings of eternal happiness is given in the text, either, but its overall emphasis is on the survival of only a relatively small number of the righteous (12.34; 13.48; cf. *T. Ab.* 11.2–12), a view which perhaps reflects the author's experience of the sweeping annihilation of Jerusalem and its inhabitants.

Ezra's questions, then, are not all answered satisfactorily by Uriel in the dialogues, but the narrative presents him as being ultimately consoled through a series of three visions, recounted in chapters 9—13. These depict a mother grieving for her only son who dies on his wedding day (9.38—10.28), an eagle which is eventually destroyed by a lion (11.1—12.3) and a figure like a man coming up out of the sea to defeat his enemies (13.1–13). The first of these revelations in particular seems to be a pivotal turning-point in converting Ezra to acceptance of some of Uriel's arguments and empowering him to offer consolation to his community (see especially 10.25–8).

These vision accounts include some traditional material and stereotypical apocalyptic features, but there may well be at least

some element of genuine religious experience underlying them.[10]
The seer prepares himself to receive these revelations by fasting
and eating only plants and flowers (9.25; 12.51; cf. 5.20; 6.31, 35),
for example, practices which were probably used at the time to induce
a state of ecstasy. They are particularly significant for what they
reveal about the messianic expectations and future hopes current
in this period. The author apparently expected an imminent end to
this world (4.50; 6.19; 7.37–8), preceded by a period of war, chaos
and other eschatological signs (5.1–13; 6.20–4; 13.31–2). Ezra, like
other first-century Jews (see e.g. Matt. 16.28; 24.3; Mark 9.1; 13.4;
Luke 17.20; 21.7; Jas. 5.7), is very curious about when exactly these
events will happen, but receives no definite information about
timings (4.51; 6.7; 8.63). He is, however, told that they will mark
the start of a period of bliss and peace or 'rest' (7.95; 8.52; cf.
Heb. 4.8–10) for the virtuous remnant. This new era is described as
being characterized especially by righteousness and truth (6.25–8;
cf. 6.49–52; 7.28, 114), but also as temporary, because it will be
succeeded by the day of judgement and the final eschatological
age (7.30–44; 12.34). At that time, the heavenly Jerusalem will be
revealed in all its glory (7.26; 8.52; 10.27, 42–4, 50–4; 13.35–6;
cf. *2 Bar.* 4.2–6; 59.4; Rev. 21.9–21), a message which would have
heartened those who had witnessed the total destruction of the
earthly city.

Some detailed explanation is given about what happens to the
souls of the dead (7.76–101; cf. 4.35; cf. *T. Ab.* 12.1–14; cf. *2 Bar.*
21.23–4; 30.2; *1 En.* 22.3–4). The final judgement is also described,
when people will be assessed on the basis of either their deeds
or their faith (e.g. 7.35, 77; 8.36; 9.7; 13.23; cf. 7.79–84), with
no apparent distinction drawn between these concepts (cf. Jas.
2.14–26).

4 Ezra is one of several writings of this period, like the *Testament
of Abraham* in particular (see above, Chapter 5), which deal with the
question of whether the righteous are able to intercede for the wicked or for their deceased relatives (7.102–3), although they give con-
tradictory answers. Uriel insists that:

---

[10] This is the view taken by Michael Stone in his *Commentary on Fourth Ezra*, for instance; see
e.g. p. 33.

Just as now a father does not send his son, or a son his father, or
a master his servant, or a friend his dearest friend, to be ill, or sleep,
or eat or be healed in his stead, so no one shall ever pray for another
then, neither shall anyone lay a burden on another; for then everyone
shall bear his own righteousness and unrighteousness ...

(7.104–5; cf. T. Ab. 14.8–14)

His answer does not convince Ezra, however, who cites several
examples of the patriarchs and prophets like Abraham and Moses
pleading successfully with God on behalf of sinners (7.106–11), to
which the angel can only respond that this traditional practice is
no longer appropriate as the end of this present age approaches
(7.112–15). This does not stop the seer himself interceding in prayer
for God's people later in the narrative (8.19–36; cf. 12.48). This issue
of individual responsibility became urgent in the light of the destruction of Jerusalem, and will also exercise the author of *2 Baruch* (e.g.
2 Bar. 54.15–19).

The Messiah is associated with the end times in three chapters
of the text, one of Uriel's speeches (7.26–44), the eagle vision (11.1–
35) and the last vision of the man arising from the sea (13.1–50),
although the term 'Messiah' is not actually used in this latter passage.
These sections draw heavily on the Scriptures, especially the
books of Daniel and Isaiah. The man-like figure is said to have
no need of weapons, for instance, since he will be able to destroy
his enemies with fiery breath from his mouth (13.9–11; cf. Isa. 11.4;
cf. *Pss. Sol.* 17.24, 33). There are some noticeable differences,
however, in the three accounts of a redeemer figure and in the functions ascribed to him. His role as a judge is more pronounced in
12.33 and 13.37–8 than in 7.28–9, for example, and the tradition
that he will reunite the 12 tribes of Israel occurs only once (13.39–47).
These variations may be due to the reuse in *4 Ezra* of traditional
material, or may simply reflect the need to employ a range of
imagery and symbolism in depicting matters which defy a full and
coherent explanation.

Nevertheless, some significant common traits do emerge. It seems
to be assumed, for example, that the Messiah is pre-existent (7.28;
12.32; 13.26, 52), that his main role is to protect and take care of
the remnant of righteous survivors (7.28; 12.34; 13.12–13, 23, 26,
48–50; cf. *2 Bar.* 29.2) and that his era is temporary (7.28–9; 12.34).

Other early Jewish sources similarly expect the messianic kingdom to be time-limited (e.g. *2 Bar.* 30.1), but *4 Ezra* is unusual in stating that he will actually die before the final day of judgement (7.29). His Davidic descent is a feature of the interpretation of the eagle vision (12.32; cf. 11.37), but is not mentioned elsewhere in the text, and no real emphasis is placed on his kingship. He does, however, have a significant role to play in pronouncing judgement on Israel's enemies, especially the Roman Empire (12.32–3; 13.37–8; cf. *2 Bar.* 39.7—40.2), which is condemned for its oppressive, arrogant and violent rule (11.32–46; 12.24), so that the whole world will be free and relieved when it has been destroyed (11.46; cf. *Sibylline Oracles* Book 5, discussed in Chapter 4, above). This fits with the overall message of *4 Ezra* that divine justice will prevail and the destruction of Jerusalem be avenged.

The redeemer figure is sometimes called God's son as well as, or instead of, Messiah (7.28–9; 13.32, 37, 52; 14.9). This title has attracted interest as possible evidence for the expectation by some first-century Jews of a divine Messiah. It may indicate Christian editing of the text, but is more likely to reflect an underlying Greek term *pais*, which can be translated either as 'son' or 'servant'. In any case, the Hebrew designation 'son of God' does not necessarily carry connotations of divinity, since it could be used of anyone who represented God or was especially close to God, like King David and his successors (e.g. 2 Sam. 7.14; Ps. 2.7). Similarly, the description of something like the figure of a man' coming up out of the sea and flying with the clouds (13.3) is usually interpreted as a deliberate echo of Daniel's vision (Dan. 7.13) rather than as a reference to a transcendent Messiah bearing the specific title 'son of man'.[11]

Despite the serious and sometimes anguished challenges which the seer is pictured as raising against traditional theological thinking, the narrative ends with him accepting that the catastrophe which has befallen Jerusalem is the result of the sin of its inhabitants and their ancestors (14.27–35), and advocating obedience to the law as the way to ensure a better future (14.22, 30; cf. 5.27; 8.12, 29; 9.31–7; 13.42, 55). Another text written at this time, *2 Baruch* (see further below), puts forward the same message, and the correct

---

[11] See esp. Stone, *Commentary on Fourth Ezra*, pp. 207–13.

interpretation and practice of the Torah will also become a central concern in rabbinic literature. While the majority of the people are urged to put their faith in the covenant promises and the keeping of the commandments, however, *4 Ezra* also claims that additional, esoteric revelation is available for the few who are able to understand it, giving them a greater insight into the wisdom of God (14.45–7; cf. 7.44; 8.62; 10.38, 57; 12.12, 36–9; 13.52–6; 14.7–9).

2 Baruch

Introduction to *2 Baruch*

This apocalypse is another theological response to the events of 70 CE.[12] As in *4 Ezra*, a figure from the time of the fall of Jerusalem to the Babylonians is chosen as the pseudonym for a text dealing with its second destruction: Baruch, son of Neriah, who is mentioned in the canonical book of Jeremiah as the prophet's secretary (Jer. 32.16; 36.4–32; 45.1; cf. 51.59). This very minor scriptural character clearly assumed considerable importance during the Second Temple period, as several later writings are attributed to him, including the apocryphal book of Baruch, *3 Baruch* and the *Paraleipomena of Jeremiah* (*4 Baruch*). Here, Baruch is depicted, like Ezra, as lamenting the fate of the people of Israel, and raising questions about God's justice and the ongoing validity of the covenant promises in the face of national catastrophe.

The narrative is located in the twenty-fifth year of King Jeconiah or Jehoiakin (1.1; see 2 Kings 24—25 which puts the exile a little earlier). This dating is an allusion to the ministry of the prophet Ezekiel, who is said to have been transported in a vision to the land of Israel 'in the twenty-fifth year of our exile' (Ezek. 40.1). *4 Ezra* opens with a similar link to Ezekiel and claims to be set 30 years after the defeat to the Babylonians, and there are so many close resemblances between *2 Baruch* and *4 Ezra* in form, structure and theology that some kind

---

[12] This has been the unanimous view of commentators to date, but a recent study has argued that it is a Christian composition; see R. Nir, *The Destruction of Jerusalem and the Idea of Redemption in the Syriac Apocalypse of Baruch*. 2003, Atlanta: SBL. This view seems impossible to defend, however, since *2 Baruch* contains no specifically Christian features, and its overriding concern is with the future of the people of Israel after the loss of their homeland and Temple in the war with Rome.

of literary relationship between the two works is usually assumed. The author of *2 Baruch* may have known and made use of *4 Ezra*, then, or both may be drawing on common sources. This time reference may even be a deliberate attempt to claim priority and greater antiquity for *2 Baruch*, although it is more likely that it is responding to *4 Ezra* than the other way round. The text was produced in the late first century CE, probably in Palestine, as Baruch is closely associated throughout with the people who have remained in the land of Israel following the deportation of much of the population (10.3; 31.2; 77.5). It is already being quoted in Christian sources by the early second century CE (e.g. 61.7 is cited in *Barn.* 11.9).

2 Baruch is only extant in full in one Syriac manuscript, Codex Ambrosianus, dated to the sixth or seventh century CE, and translated from Greek. One fragment containing parts of chapters 12—14 in Greek was discovered among the Oxyrhynchus Papyri in Egypt, and there is also a single copy of an Arabic version, based on the Syriac. The original language was almost certainly Hebrew, however, as the Syriac is virtually unintelligible in places, and becomes clearer after translation into Hebrew. The final part of the work, a letter from Baruch to the exiles of the Northern Kingdom summarizing much of the earlier material (chapters 78—87), was evidently transmitted independently, as it is attested in over 30 further Syriac manuscripts. This section may, therefore, either have been composed by a different author and incorporated into the book later, or, more probably, become detached from it over time. Its contents fit with the overall themes of *2 Baruch*, and it is presumably intended to correspond to the letter which was reportedly sent by Jeremiah from Jerusalem to the exiles in Babylon (Jer. 29.1–28).

As well as the marked affinities with *4 Ezra*, there are numerous connections with another text from this period, the *Biblical Antiquities* of Pseudo-Philo (see above, Chapter 2), including the employment of traditions about Adam and Moses enjoying heavenly visions (4.3–5; cf. *L.A.B.* 19.10; 26.6), and the description of a place where the dead are kept until the final judgement (23.4–5; cf. *L.A.B.* 3.10; *1 En.* 22.3–5). Notable parallels can also be observed in wording and ideas with some New Testament writings, especially the Pauline letters, which likewise emerged from within the same historical, religious and geographical context.

Key features of *2 Baruch*

2 Baruch is a lengthy text containing several different literary forms, including speeches and dialogues, visions and revelations, prayers and laments, and a letter. Its structure is difficult to determine, with some commentators dividing it into seven episodes, in line with the arrangement of *4 Ezra*.[13] Only three major sections are really clearly defined, however: a Prologue (chapters 1—9) setting the scene for the narrative at the time of the Babylonian exile; the main body of the work (chapters 10—77), which includes dialogues between Baruch and God about the reasons for the destruction of Jerusalem and consoling revelations about the future of Israel; and a letter from Baruch to the exiles in Assyria (chapters 78—87).

One vision appears to have particular significance, and depicts a cloud appearing out of the sea and pouring out over the earth water, which is alternately dark and bright in colour. This vision report and its detailed interpretation (chapters 53—76) make up about one third of the whole text, and offer the same kind of symbolic and periodized representation of Israel's history (see also 27.1—28.2; 42.6) as the Animal Apocalypse (*1 En.* 85—90) and Apocalypse of Weeks (*1 En.* 93.1–10; 91.11–17). The author clearly draws throughout on a range of pre-existing apocalyptic sources and themes, sometimes shaping them to fit his particular purposes. He introduces a four-kingdom historical scheme into his explanation of a vision of a vine and a cedar tree (39.1–5), for example, even though this motif is not present in the actual revelation (36.1—37.1). He is also familiar with the developments of the Genesis account of angels taking human women as wives (56.10–14; cf. Gen. 6.1–4) which are widely employed in the Enochic literature (e.g. *1 En.* 6.1—10.14; 86.1–6), but in his somewhat different reading of this tradition, the angels' fall is blamed on Adam (56.10).

Baruch is not taken on any heavenly journeys, but, interestingly, he does enjoy extensive direct communication with God, so that the mediation of an interpreting angel is not such a prominent feature in this text as in other apocalyptic writings, although the angel Ramiel does disclose the meaning of the vision of the waters (55.3). Such

---

[13] See e.g. F. J. Murphy, *Apocalypticism in the Bible and Its World.* 2012, Grand Rapids, Michigan: Baker Academic, pp. 151–9.

immediate divine access may have been considered appropriate for Baruch, who is presented as the chosen successor to God's prophet and messenger Jeremiah (e.g. 10.1; 33.1–2), or it may be a deliberate attempt to enhance his authority and trustworthiness as a teacher. *2 Baruch* is also rooted in the narrative and language of Scripture, and frequently alludes to Jeremiah and the books of the Deuteronomistic History, especially 2 Kings and 2 Chronicles. In general, it follows the Deuteronomistic evaluation of Israel's kings, idealizing, for instance, the time of David and Solomon (61.1–8) and enhancing the wickedness of Manasseh (64.7–9; cf. *b. Sanh.* 103b), but, in agreement with Josephus, is rather more positive about Jehoiachin (1.3; cf. 2 Kings 24.9; *Ant.* 10.100; *J.W.* 6.106). There are also important echoes of Deuteronomy, such as reminders that through the covenant and the commandments God has offered the Israelites the choice between life and death (19.1; 84.1–5; cf. Deut. 30.15–20).

Important themes in *2 Baruch*

In common with *4 Ezra* and other writings from this time, *2 Baruch* is ultimately concerned with the question of whether the Roman destruction of Jerusalem signals the end of God's special relationship with Israel. Its consoling message is that, despite appearances to the contrary, the covenant promises are still effective, and will be fulfilled for those Israelites who remain faithful to the law. This teaching is given weight through its ascription to an authoritative figure who witnessed at first hand a previous national disaster. Baruch is no longer a secretary, but replaces Jeremiah as God's prophet and spokesperson for those who remain in Jerusalem after Jeremiah is sent to Babylon (10.2–3; cf. 33.2). This picture does not tally with the scriptural account that both Jeremiah and Baruch went to Egypt during the exile (Jer. 43.6–7). According to this text, however, it is to Baruch that God's word now comes (1.1; 10.1) so that he might pass it on to others, including Jeremiah (2.1; 10.2; cf. 5.5; 9.1), and, like Ezekiel, he is lifted up by God's spirit and shown visions (6.1—7.1). He is in fact comparable also to Moses, the greatest prophet and teacher of the law, as he intercedes on behalf of the people (e.g. 21.20–5; 48.11–24), receives revelations in a 40-day period on a mountain (76.4), and calls his community to renewed observance of the commandments (e.g. 41.3–4; 77.6). This portrayal of the apocalyptic seer as a prophet like Moses is a further example of the relationship between *4 Ezra* and *2 Baruch* (see *4 Ezra* 14.1–3, 42–5), and resonates with the presentation of Jesus as a new Moses in the Gospel of Matthew.

Although *4 Ezra* and *2 Baruch* employ similar forms and themes in responding to the loss of the land and the Temple, *4 Ezra* is generally recognized as the more daring in its questioning of both God and traditional theological positions, and Baruch's distress and grief at the plight of the people does not appear as profound as Ezra's. This is at least in part because at the very beginning of this narrative he receives a full explanation of the reasons for the disaster, and reassurance about Israel's future, which provides a different context for his subsequent dialogues with God. The first exile, and, by implication, the second fall of Jerusalem, are firmly attributed to the sin of the people throughout this text, but the audience learns from the outset that this punishment will be only a temporary 'chastening', after which they can look forward to a prosperous future (1.5; cf. 13.9–10; 78.5; 79.3). This language is reminiscent of the justification for the suffering of the righteous offered in the *Psalms of Solomon* (e.g. *Pss. Sol.* 10.1–3; 13.7–9; 14.1; 16.11; see above, Chapter 4).

The destruction should not, therefore, be viewed as a victory for God's enemies, but as the action of God (6.4—8.2; cf. 80.1–3), and it clearly demonstrates that no individual or nation can escape punishment for sin, including Israel:

> You who have drunk the clarified wine will now drink its dregs, for the judgement of the Most High is impartial. Therefore, he did not spare his own sons first, but he afflicted them as his enemies because they sinned. Therefore, they were once punished, that they might be forgiven. But now, you nations and tribes, you are guilty . . .
>
> (13.3–11; 82.1–9; cf. Wisd. 12.20–22; 2 Macc. 7.18–19)[14]

The future of God's chosen people is assured, however, so the audience can be confident that, if they remain faithful to the law, they will be restored (44.7; 46.5; 54.14; 84.1–11; 85.4). As

---

[14] All translations of the text are taken from A. F. J. Klijn, '2 (Syriac Apocalypse of) Baruch'. In *The Old Testament Pseudepigrapha Vol. 1*. Ed. J. H. Charlesworth. 1983, New York: Doubleday, pp. 615–52.

in other texts of the time, no distinction is drawn here between keeping the commandments or 'works' and believing or having 'faith' (51.7; 54.5, 21; cf. *4 Ezra* 7.35, 77–84; 8.36; 9.7; 13.23; Jas. 2.14–26).

The author of *2 Baruch* seems to have been fully aware of the challenges to God's justice raised in *4 Ezra*, especially the claim that people are not totally culpable for their wrongdoing after Adam's sin, and the criticism of God for condemning the vast majority of human beings to eternal suffering. He explicitly disagrees, therefore, with the position that only a few people will be able to keep the law and therefore achieve salvation: 'while many have sinned once, many others have proved themselves to be righteous' (21.11; cf. *4 Ezra* 7.46–8, 60–1). He also stresses individual responsibility and freedom of choice, while still accepting that all subsequent human beings have been deeply affected by Adam's actions (23.4; 48.42–3; 56.5–8; cf. *4 Ezra* 3.20–6; 4.28–32; 7.118):

> For, although Adam sinned first and has brought death upon all who were not in his own time, yet each of them who has been born from him has prepared for himself the coming torment. And further, each of them has chosen for himself the coming glory . . . Adam is, therefore, not the cause, except only for himself, but each of us has become our own Adam . . . (54.15–19)

It is possible that in passages such as these the author is deliberately seeking to tone down some of the more radical statements found in *4 Ezra*.

An important theme of *2 Baruch* is that the covenant promises have not been broken, but their fulfilment has been transferred to the eschatological age. As in *4 Ezra*, the end of the present world is envisaged as being imminent, with the days now advancing more rapidly than in the past (20.1; 85.10; cf. *4 Ezra* 4.26; 5.50–5; *L.A.B.* 19.3), although no definite time indications are given. It will be preceded by signs and tribulations (25.2–3; 48.32–7; 70.3–8; cf. *4 Ezra* 5.1–13; 8.63—9.6; *1 En.* 99.4–5; *Sib. Or.* 3.796–808; Matt. 24.3–8; Mark 13.4–8; Luke 21.7–11). Then the pre-existent Messiah will be revealed (29.2; cf. 70.9), and his coming will mark the complete renewal of Creation: 'on one vine will be a thousand branches, and one branch will produce a thousand clusters, and one cluster will produce a thousand grapes, and one grape will produce a cor of wine' (29.5; cf. *1 En.* 10.19). The messianic era will be temporary (30.1; cf. 40.3), and will be followed by the resurrection of the righteous (30.1–4) and the dawning of the final new age, which will be eternal (44.11–13), and in which all the scriptural hopes for happiness and peace will be realized (73.1—74.3; cf. e.g. Isa. 11.6–9).

Some interest is shown in the state of souls after death (21.23–4; 30.2; cf. *4 Ezra* 4.35; 7.76–101; *T. Ab.* 12.1–14; *1 En.* 22.3–4), and particularly in the question of whether the human body will take on a changed appearance in the future world, a subject which is known to have exercised the early Christian community in Corinth also (49.1—51.16; cf. 1 Cor. 15.35–57). According to *2 Baruch*, the dead will initially be able to recognize one another (50.2–4), but then the righteous 'will be glorified by transformations' (51.3) and become like the angels or the stars, while the wicked will acquire a more horrible form (51.1–11).

The Messiah features in this author's eschatological thinking, but he does not play a particularly significant part in it. No extensive or detailed role is set out for him, for instance, and he is not referred to in large parts of the text, or even in every description of the end times (see e.g. 85.10–15). The main function ascribed to him is the judgement and destruction of the kingdom of Rome (39.7—40.2; cf. *4 Ezra* 12.32–3; 13.37–8), and of all the nations which have oppressed Israel (72.2–6). This minimizing of messianic expectation is interpreted by commentators such as Frederick Murphy as part of a warning that vengeance against the Romans should be left to God and not enacted by the people through a further armed rebellion.[15] This is not a particularly striking theme in the text, but might be suggested in these verses: 'For why do you look for the decline of your enemies? Prepare your souls for that which is kept for you' (52.6–7).

It is the future fate of the covenant people, not of humanity as a whole, which is the major concern of *2 Baruch*. Only those found in the land of Israel will be protected at the time of the coming of the Messiah (29.2), for example, and 'mingling with the nations'

---

[15] F. J. Murphy, *The Structure and Meaning of 2 Baruch.* 1985, Atlanta: Scholars Press.

is condemned (42.4; 48.23) because they are generally considered wicked and unrighteous (13.11–12; 62.7). The concluding letter also expresses a hope for the eventual reunification of all 12 tribes (78.7; cf. *4 Ezra* 13.12, 40, 47). Nevertheless, it is made clear that gentiles who have not harmed God's people will be spared in the final judgement (72.4–5), and that proselytes can be included in the future salvation, while Israelites who choose not to keep the commandments will be excluded from it (42.1; 42.8). In answering the question 'Who will be saved?', then, this author subtly redefines the meaning of 'Israel' so that it relates to observance of the law and is no longer a strictly ethnic entity.

A further issue treated here is the place of the Temple in the end times. Like other texts from the late Second Temple period, *2 Baruch* assumes the existence of a heavenly counterpart to the earthly Jerusalem (4.2–6; 59.4; cf. Wisd. 9.8; Gal. 4.6; Heb. 8.5), but there is no emphasis on the restoration of the Temple in the messianic age (cf. *1 En.* 90.34–6). This may reflect some dissatisfaction on the part of the circles behind the work with the Second Temple and its cult. The priests of the First Temple are criticized for their poor stewardship of God's house (10.18), for instance, in a comment which may have been directed also at those who had ministered in the Second Temple, which is specifically said to have been less successful in attracting the honour of gentiles than its predecessor (68.6). However, it is also possible that the author simply chooses not to dwell extensively on this subject because the members of his community are still coming to terms with the destruction of their 'mother' Jerusalem (3.1–3; 10.16; cf. *4 Ezra* 10.7; Gal. 4.26), so need to find consolation by focusing not on the institutions of the past, but on the world to come.

Faced with the loss of the national homeland and the end of traditional forms of Temple worship, the rabbis would reconstruct Judaism around the proper interpretation and full observance of the Torah. *2 Baruch* similarly puts the Mosaic law at the heart of its ethical instruction and message of hope for the future: 'Also we have left our land, and Zion has been taken away from us, and we have nothing now apart from the mighty one and his law' (85.3; cf. e.g. 38.1–4; 46.5; 48.25; 59.2; 77.16; 84.1–10). Here, however, this covenantal theological approach is reconciled with a belief in the need for additional apocalyptic revelations, but there is no sense that any of this material is secret or reserved for a small circle of the wise (cf. *4 Ezra* 14.45–7), or that Baruch faces opposition to his views (see e.g. 5.5; 31.1–2; 32.8–9; 44.1; 46.1–3; 76.5; 77.12). This particular apocalypse at least, then, does not seem to be the product of a marginalized or alienated group.

Other examples of apocalyptic literature

This genre is well attested within Scripture itself, both in the Hebrew Bible (e.g. Daniel, Joel, Zechariah), and in the New Testament (e.g. Mark 13 and parallels; 1 and 2 Thessalonians; Revelation). Apocalyptic writings continued to be produced and circulated within early Christianity, including a particularly popular work from the early second century CE, the *Shepherd of Hermas*, which deals with the themes of sin, repentance and forgiveness. No new apocalypses have been discovered at Qumran, although an eschatological and dualistic world-view similar to that characteristic of apocalyptic writings is present in much of the sectarian literature, for example in the *War Scroll* (1QM).

There is one further text which might have been included in this chapter, an originally Jewish work called the *Apocalypse of Abraham*. It is omitted here because its date is uncertain, so it may fall outside the Second Temple period, and it also shows unmistakable signs of Christian editing (e.g. 29.3–14). In it, Abraham is taken by an angel on a heavenly journey (chapters 15—29) where he sees God's throne (17.1—18.14) and experiences other visions, including a final judgement scene (21.7). Like the other apocalypses, this one, too, is concerned to explain the presence in the world of evil, especially the prevalence of idolatry.

The significance of apocalyptic literature

It is not difficult to make a case for the continuing significance of the apocalyptic literature, given the regular appearance of groups and individuals heavily influenced by its outlook who claim to be able to calculate the precise date of the end of the world. Perhaps, however, in view of these popular associations of apocalyptic thought with misplaced speculation about the future, fanaticism and weird symbolism, it is particularly important to understand this literature more fully and reach a better appreciation of its breadth and underlying purposes. This survey of the major Jewish apocalypses from the Second Temple period has demonstrated, for instance, that its visionary language is not intended to baffle or frighten its audience, but to offer a consoling and intelligible message, rooted in contemporary experience. The marked emphasis on the theme of impending judgement can then be seen as part of an overall message of reassurance about God's justice, control of world history, and profound concern for those who are enduring suffering and oppression.

Some examples of this genre emerged in times of political, social and religious crisis, such as during the Hellenistic reform programme of Antiochus IV Epiphanes (e.g. the Animal Apocalypse and the Book of the Watchers in *1 Enoch*) or in the aftermath of the total destruction of Jerusalem by the Romans (*4 Ezra, 2 Baruch*). Apocalyptic writings were not all composed in such difficult circumstances, however, and the particular significance of *1 Enoch* lies in the fact that, as a collection of texts spanning at least three centuries, it clearly illustrates an ongoing process of engagement with a long-established tradition, thereby illuminating the development of the apocalyptic genre over time.

The apocalypses considered in this chapter provide further evidence of the breadth of thought current in the Second Temple period, attesting, especially in the case of *1 Enoch* (cf. parts of *4 Ezra*), to a form of Judaism which was less centred on the Mosaic law and the covenant than that which became dominant in the rabbinic period, and which included a mystical dimension. This literature has contributed, therefore, to disproving the view once propounded by many Christians that early Judaism was a narrow and legalistic religion. Nowhere is this diversity of thought clearer than in the remarkable variety of messianic expectation reflected in these writings. In the light of the descriptions of a heavenly son of man redeemer figure (Similitudes of Enoch, *4 Ezra* 13), similar to the presentation of Jesus in Matthew's Gospel, a Messiah who is called God's son or servant (*4 Ezra* 7.28–9; 13.32, 37, 52; 14.9) and even a Messiah who dies before the final inauguration of God's kingdom (*4 Ezra* 7.29), it has now become impossible to continue to accept the once widely held claim that all first-century Jews expected a Davidic warrior Messiah.

The apocalyptic writings are recognized, then, as providing essential information about the thought-world of early Christianity, and several interesting parallels between these texts and parts of the New Testament have been identified in this chapter. These include a shared interest in the effect on subsequent human beings of Adam's disobedience and in the question of who will be saved and on what basis, a common expectation of the establishment of a restored Jerusalem on earth and a similar presentation of an authoritative teacher as a new Moses figure.

The authors of these apocalypses tackled very deep questions which continue to concern people today, such as the origins of evil, the extent of human responsibility for sin, and the proper religious response to human suffering. Their treatment of these issues is often creative and thought-provoking, as they are willing to challenge traditional theologies. It is, for example, particularly important to appreciate that some early Jewish traditions do not emphasize Adam's 'fall', and that the picture of salvation given in these texts usually centres on a renewed earth, not its destruction and a mass transfer of humanity to the heavenly world (see e.g. *1 En.* 10.18—11.2; *2 Bar.* 29.5). As already noted, this outlook can be used to promote a sense of stewardship of Creation, and a greater engagement in political and social action. It is reflected, for instance, in strong condemnation of those who practise injustice, especially the rulers and extremely wealthy classes (e.g. *1 En.* 62.1—63.12; cf. *4 Ezra* 11.32–46; 12.24).

Further reading

Collins, J. J., *The Apocalyptic Imagination: An Introduction to Jewish Apocalyptic Literature*. 2nd edn. 1998, Grand Rapids, Michigan/Cambridge, UK: Eerdmans

Hogan, K. M., *Theologies in Conflict in 4 Ezra: Wisdom Debate and Apocalyptic Solution*. 2008, Leiden: Brill

Longenecker, B. W., *2 Esdras*. 1995, Sheffield: Sheffield Academic Press

Murphy, F. J., *Apocalypticism in the Bible and Its World*. 2012, Grand Rapids, Michigan: Baker Academic

Nickelsburg, G. W. E. and Vanderkam, J. C., *1 Enoch: A New Translation.* 2004, Minneapolis: Fortress Press

Oegema, G. S., *Apocalyptic Interpretation of the Bible.* 2012, London: T&T Clark

Sayler, G. B., *Have the Promises Failed? A Literary Analysis of 2 Baruch.* 1984, Chico, California: Scholars Press

Stone, M. E., *Fourth Ezra: A Commentary on the Book of Fourth Ezra.* 1990, Minneapolis: Fortress Press

7

Conclusions

In this review of the Pseudepigrapha, central theological themes have been highlighted, and attention has been drawn to their noteworthy literary features. The historical context of each text has been considered, and appropriate connections made with the wider body of early Jewish literature. It has also been argued throughout that these writings continue to have significance for readers today. They are, first, interesting as literary creations in their own right, which entertain, move and inform their readers. Their enduring value lies also in the evidence which they provide about the history, beliefs and practices of Jews in the Second Temple period; in what they reveal about the relationship between the emerging religions of Judaism and Christianity in the early centuries CE; in the ancient interpretations which they preserve of the texts now accepted by Jews and Christians as authoritative Scripture; and in the theological and ethical teaching which they put forward, some of which may continue to be applicable in the twenty-first century. This final chapter will offer some concluding reflections on the main issues which have emerged from this study of the pseudepigraphical literature.

Use of Scripture

All the Pseudepigrapha stand in a very close relationship to the books which now form the Jewish Scriptures. Their authors all presuppose the biblical narrative, and take for granted its truth, ongoing relevance and centrality for their religious identity. They demonstrate complete familiarity with all parts of the Scriptures, from the Pentateuchal narratives and laws, through the various accounts of Israel's history and the prophetic oracles, to the Psalms and other wisdom writings. They rarely actually cite biblical texts or comment formally on them, but, to a greater or lesser extent, all of them are engaged in interpreting the Scriptures and re-presenting their teaching. So the language of the Scriptures is widely echoed and imitated, in both narratives like *Jubilees* and liturgical texts like the *Psalms of Solomon*; its literary forms are employed, including hymns, oracles and testaments; and new stories, like the tale told in *Joseph and Aseneth*, are set against its backdrop.

This serious and pervasive engagement with the Scriptures illustrates the authority which these particular writings had already attained in the Second Temple period, but the level of freedom and creativity with which these later authors approach them is also striking. The underlying biblical narrative can, therefore, be supplemented with additional details which fill in perceived gaps, or abbreviated so that incidents now considered unedifying can be glossed over. It can even be contradicted, both in terms of small details such as the age of a patriarch or the location of an episode, and in more substantial ways, such as in the reformulation of the characters of Abraham and Job in the testaments attributed to them. The authors of the Pseudepigrapha appear to have been motivated above all by the goal of making these traditional texts relevant and intelligible to the people of their time. This is achieved by, for example, updating prophetic and apocalyptic oracles for different circumstances, rewriting Scripture to address contemporary concerns, or expressing it in a form more accessible to a Graeco-Roman audience, such as through a drama like the *Exagoge* or a novella like *Joseph and Aseneth*. Close study of the Pseudepigrapha clearly reveals that these Second Temple Jews did not approach their authoritative writings as a set of fixed, unchanging letters on a page. Rather, communicating the meaning of this revelation for future generations seems to have been more important to them than its precise wording or form; so, for example, the biblical narrative can be literally rewritten, and new psalms and oracles can be composed. This concern to relate the Scriptures to present-day issues and convey traditional teaching in imaginative ways perhaps has its modern equivalents in developments such as inclusive-language Bible translations or the composition of rap songs with a religious message.

The extensive use of Scripture in these early Jewish texts also illustrates the historical development of interpretative traditions which are employed in later rabbinic or early Christian sources, and provides further evidence of the variety of forms in which the

Scriptures circulated in this period before the Masoretic version became standard. In, for example, *Jubilees*, the *Biblical Antiquities* and the *Testament of Job*, a different underlying text is often reflected, one closer to the form of the Septuagint or the Samaritan Pentateuch.

Diversity of Second Temple Judaism

The most important lesson learned from reading the Pseudepigrapha is a deeper appreciation of the richness and diversity of early Judaism. It is especially significant that so many of the writings considered in this volume originated in the Diaspora. This is the context in which the great majority of Jews lived during the Second Temple period, but their experience does not always receive sufficient attention, since it is not fully reflected in the scriptural writings. This volume has demonstrated that, although texts composed in Palestine, such as the *Testament of Moses*, the *Biblical Antiquities* or *4 Ezra*, are characterized by some distinctive features, they also share a great many beliefs, ethical values and exegetical traditions in common with those produced in the Diaspora. The role played by historical, geographical and social context in shaping theology cannot be underestimated and so, for instance, a greater emphasis on the uniqueness of Israel and the ongoing validity of the covenant is evident in the Palestinian writings, and particular concerns such as the conduct of Temple worship, or responses to the Roman invasion of Judaea, do surface in them. However, there is no marked difference from the Diaspora works in the understanding of what it means to live a good life, for example, and themes such as a strong commitment to monotheism and to social justice are present in texts from different locations.

Some quite unexpected commonalities across geographical boundaries also emerge from a close investigation of the Pseudepigrapha, such as the possible evidence for a belief among the Diaspora communities represented by *Joseph and Aseneth* and the *Testament of Job* that human beings can participate in angelic life, similar to the view attested in the literature discovered at Qumran. It is also interesting to find Palestinian texts which were probably composed originally in Greek, not Hebrew (e.g. *Testament of Moses*), demonstrating the extent of Hellenistic influence in Israel. Above all, the Pseudepigrapha provide evidence of the variety of belief and practice which was permissible within Second Temple Judaism. The fact that, for instance, it is difficult to definitely attribute any of these writings to known groups, such as the Pharisees or Essenes, demonstrates the breadth of early Jewish life and thought, and a mystical strand which is not always acknowledged in accounts of this period is also evident in several of these writings (e.g. *Exagoge, Joseph and Aseneth, Testament of Job, 1 Enoch, 4 Ezra*). This is an important counterbalance to the once widely held view, now disproved by scholarship, that Judaism in the early centuries BCE and CE was a narrow and legalistic form of religion.

The understanding of Judaism in this period is enhanced especially by a consideration, first, of the attitude taken in the Pseudepigrapha towards gentiles and Hellenistic culture. In several of these texts, there is evidence that at least some Diaspora Jews felt at home in Graeco-Roman society, had been influenced by Greek education, philosophy and literature, and were keen to find common ground with their gentile fellow-citizens. *Joseph and Aseneth* and the *Exagoge* in particular seem to reflect positive relationships between Jews and gentiles, and in the *Sibylline Oracles* pagan, Jewish and Christian elements are intriguingly combined. There is also very little to distinguish the ethical teaching of the *Testaments of the Twelve Patriarchs* from the general moral norms of the wider community. A particularly open and universalistic outlook is also found in the *Testament of Abraham*, where no clear distinction is made between Jews and gentiles, who will all be judged on the basis of their deeds by Abel, the son of Adam who was regarded as the father of all humanity. These writings can be viewed, then, as early examples of the attempt to 'inculturate' Jewish theology and actively engage with the contemporary society, and so they offer a particular perspective on an issue which continues to be a matter of debate within several of the world's religions.

Second, the Pseudepigrapha are particularly important for the light they shed on the religious and cultural context from which early Christianity emerged. This volume has highlighted repeatedly the difficulty of drawing hard and fast distinctions between 'Judaism' and 'Christianity' in the first two or three centuries of the Common Era. This is evidenced, for instance, in the fact that works like the

Testament of Job or *The Life of Adam and Eve* could have been produced in either Christian or Jewish circles. A further interesting example of this point is the diversity of messianic thought reflected in this literature. A Messiah figure does not feature prominently at all in the eschatological scenario painted in some of these texts, and in others a variety of future saviours are described with no attempt at harmonization (e.g. *Sibylline Oracles, 4 Ezra, Testaments of the Twelve Patriarchs*). Only the *Psalms of Solomon* attests to a clear and detailed expectation of a Davidic warrior Messiah, although there are some elements of this picture elsewhere, in parts of *4 Ezra* and the *Testaments of the Twelve Patriarchs*, for instance. Some authors await the coming of a priestly Messiah (e.g. *Testament of Levi*), or a pre-existent heavenly figure related to the 'one like a son of man' in Daniel's vision (Dan. 7.13; e.g. *4 Ezra, 1 Enoch*). In the mysterious Taxo, the *Testament of Moses* may present an alternative view that the martyrdom of a righteous Israelite will prompt God's saving intervention. These writings, therefore, offer extremely interesting comparative material for the use of the term 'son of man' in the Gospels, for the high priestly Christology of Hebrews and for early Christian teaching about the sinless Jesus' willingness to accept death on behalf of others.

Further interesting thematic and literary connections between the New Testament and the Pseudepigrapha have also been highlighted in this volume, such as: parallels between the infancy narratives and the account of the birth of Moses in the *Biblical Antiquities*; the similar hope for the restoration on earth of a new and glorious Jerusalem in the book of Revelation and apocalyptic and sibylline literature; and the presentation of Jesus as a new Moses in the Gospel of Matthew, echoing the portrayal of Ezra and Baruch in the late first-century apocalypses bearing their names. Other theological developments within Second Temple Judaism attested in these books are likewise reflected in the New Testament, including debates about the continuing effects of Adam's sin (e.g. *4 Ezra, 2 Baruch*) or the possibility of salvation for gentiles (e.g. *Sibylline Oracles, 1 Enoch, 2 Baruch*). Aspects of early Christian ethical teaching also prove to be part of a wider Jewish tradition, for example the exhortation to leave behind worldly goods in order to gain something better in heaven (*Joseph and Aseneth, Testament of Job*). The Pseudepigrapha, then, provide essential information about the background of thought to the New Testament.

Theological themes

Finally, the Pseudepigrapha are significant for the answers which they give to deep questions of ongoing relevance, such as how to deal with innocent suffering (e.g. *Psalms of Solomon, 4 Ezra*), how to deal with the fear of death (e.g. *Testament of Abraham*) or how sin came into the world (e.g. *The Life of Adam and Eve, 1 Enoch*). The authors of these texts are often thoughtful and creative thinkers, who are not afraid to challenge traditional explanations. The *Psalms of Solomon*, for example, shows a devout Jewish community whose members are not totally satisfied with the traditional explanation that suffering is a consequence of sin, and who therefore introduce a distinction between God's punishment of the wicked and a cleansing fatherly discipline for the righteous. The seer in *4 Ezra* goes even beyond this in his daring questioning of God's justice and commitment to the covenant. This kind of anguished refusal to complacently accept conventional responses to the loss of faith caused by the Roman destruction of Jerusalem would be needed again by Jewish theologians in their attempts to deal with the even greater horror of the Holocaust.

The authors of the Pseudepigrapha generally sought to offer consolation to their audiences in difficult circumstances and to calm their fears, stressing, for example, that God's mercy is boundless (*Testament of Abraham*), that human beings are made in God's image (*The Life of Adam and Eve*) and that God's righteousness will ultimately prevail over evil, if only in the end times (*1 Enoch*). The contemporary reader, too, may find something of value in their teaching about issues which are as important now as they were two millennia ago. Several of the Pseudepigrapha are also uncompromising in their scathing criticism of oppressive political and religious elites, whether Jewish or gentile, and of all forms of injustice (e.g. *Psalms of Solomon, Sibylline Oracles, 1 Enoch*). At times their language borders on the subversive, and it offers an important reminder of the long history of social critique and political engagement inspired by the scriptural teaching on justice.

Future directions

The Pseudepigrapha will continue to be a valuable resource for those engaged in biblical studies, textual criticism, and the study of early Judaism and early Christianity. They are also of considerable interest to feminist scholars, because of the added prominence given in several of the texts (e.g. *Joseph and Aseneth, Testament of Job, Biblical Antiquities*) to women characters, which illuminates not only early biblical interpretation, but also the question of the place of women in Graeco-Roman society and in Second Temple Judaism.

Pressing questions for future scholarship remain, including the need for further investigation into the boundaries and origins of several of the genres employed in this literature, especially rewritten Scripture and apocalyptic. The issue of the Jewish or Christian provenance of many of these texts is also far from settled, and the development of a methodology for reaching decisions about this is only in the very early stages. As a consequence of further research in this area, it is very likely that writings such as the *Testaments of the Twelve Patriarchs* or the *Ascension of Isaiah* will assume greater importance as witnesses to the beliefs and practices of Christians in the early centuries of the Common Era, a time for which extant written sources are scarce. To return to a claim made in the Introduction to this volume, the fact that the Pseudepigrapha, originally Jewish writings, were all transmitted and evidently valued in Christian circles, and were sometimes, as in the case of *4 Ezra* and the *Testaments of the Twelve Patriarchs*, incorporated into new Christian works, is an important reminder of the shared scriptural, theological and literary heritage of these two religions. A better appreciation of this reality can only strengthen relationships between Jews and Christians today and serve to advance interfaith dialogue.

Index of ancient sources

Index of modern authors

Index of subjects

Abraham 8, 16, 17, 19, 22, 23, 24, 25, 26,
30, 33, 75, 105, 115–21, 123, 137, 145,
155, 160
Adam and Eve 18, 20, 22, 23, 27, 34, 38,
50–8, 59, 60, 120, 127, 131, 132, 135,
136, 142, 148, 149, 152, 157, 162, 163
Alexander the Great 4, 6, 80, 87
Ancient of Days 67, 129
angels 15, 17, 19, 20, 22, 29, 31–2, 36, 39, 43,
46–7, 48, 51, 54, 57, 59, 82, 90, 99, 103, 105,
107, 108, 113, 115, 117, 118, 119, 120, 122,
125, 126, 129, 130, 131, 134, 135, 139, 141,
145, 149, 153, 155, 161
Antiochus IV Epiphanes 4, 14, 19, 21, 108, 109,
129, 135, 137, 156
apocalypse 2 n. 1, 9, 17, 32, 82, 110, 125, 126,
135, 137, 139, 141, 147, 155, 156, 157, 163
Apocalypse of Abraham 155
apocalyptic 9, 17, 28, 29, 38, 54, 59, 67 n. 4,
73, 80, 82, 86, 93, 94, 99, 102, 103, 109,
110, 117, 119, 124, 125–58, 160, 163, 165
Apocrypha 1, 2, 10, 38, 58, 137, 147
Aramaic Levi Document 15, 94, 99
Ascension of Isaiah 58–9, 94, 165

Babylon 2, 4, 6, 70, 75, 82, 85, 88, 137, 138,
139, 142, 147, 148, 149, 150
baptism 3, 40, 47, 56, 91
2 Baruch 6, 24, 32, 145, 146, 147–55, 156, 163
Beliar 22, 99
Benjamin 50, 94
Biblical Antiquities 16, 19, 23–33, 34–7, 41,
75, 112, 121, 148, 161, 163, 165
Bilhah 96, 98, 99

Cain and Abel 27, 53, 57, 76, 116, 119, 120,
132, 162
calendar, solar/lunar 15, 21, 135
Canaan 19, 39, 64, 68, 108
Christianity, early 1, 3, 10, 12, 13, 35, 36, 39, 40,
42, 46, 47, 48, 52, 54, 56, 58–9, 60–1, 62, 70,
78, 79–81, 87, 90, 93, 94, 96, 97, 99–100, 101,
107, 114, 116, 118, 121, 122, 129, 133, 134,
137–8, 142, 146, 147 n. 12, 148, 153, 155,
157, 159, 160, 162–3, 164
circumcision 6, 7, 18, 20, 22, 35, 69, 96, 116
conversion 8, 18, 39, 40, 41, 42, 45, 46, 48,
49, 61, 85
covenant 14, 15, 17, 18, 19, 23, 24, 26, 28, 29,
30, 31, 35, 36, 75, 111, 112, 113, 114, 121,
122, 128, 130, 141, 142, 147, 150, 152, 153,

154, 156, 161, 164
creation 16, 18, 19, 20, 21, 22, 23, 29, 35, 80,
83, 112, 113, 129, 130, 131, 132, 133, 135,
136, 139, 140, 143, 152, 157

Dan 39, 50, 60, 98
Daniel, book of 89, 135, 145, 155
David 5, 23, 24, 27, 28, 29, 32, 50, 70, 71,
76, 77, 78, 91, 97, 134, 146, 150, 157, 163
Dead Sea Scrolls 1, 10, 15, 21, 33, 71, 78, 92,
107 n. 9, 140 n. 8
Deborah 25, 26, 28, 36
determinism 112, 126, 139
Deuteronomistic History 31, 75, 150
Deuteronomy, book of 12, 31, 67, 89, 108,
110, 111, 150
devil 53, 54, 56, 57, 104, 106, 113; *see also* Satan
Diaspora 6–8, 9, 10, 11, 38, 40, 44, 62, 63,
68, 69, 76, 83, 86 n. 13, 86 n. 14, 87, 90,
91, 92, 101, 109, 120, 124, 161, 162
dietary regulations, Jewish 6, 7, 96, 116
Dinah 18, 35, 41, 98, 105

Eden, Garden of 18, 22, 51, 53, 57, 133
Egypt/Egyptians 6, 7, 8, 16, 21, 24, 28, 30,
33, 34, 39, 40, 41, 44, 45, 46, 48, 49, 50, 60,
63, 64, 65, 66, 67, 68, 70, 79, 80, 82, 83, 86,
87, 88, 92, 98, 101, 107, 116, 135, 148, 150;
see also Pharaoh
Enoch 1, 8, 17, 20, 95, 121, 125, 127–37
1 Enoch 1, 8, 17–18, 109, 125, 127–37, 139,
156–8, 162, 163, 164
Enochic literature/tradition 21, 51, 95, 121,
122, 127–37, 149
Esau 16, 17, 22
eschatology 17, 32, 57, 73, 76–8, 79, 80, 83,
85, 87, 88, 93, 96–7, 101, 108, 110, 112, 114,
126, 136, 141, 144, 145–6, 152–4, 155, 163
Essenes 5, 14, 47, 91, 101, 128, 162
ethical teaching 9, 10, 38, 50, 56, 61, 62, 79,
84–5, 86–7, 93, 94, 95, 96, 101, 107, 110,
116, 128, 130, 137, 154, 159, 161, 162, 163
Eucharist 3, 40, 47
Exagoge, The 1, 62–9, 81, 90–2, 160, 162
exile, Babylonian 2, 4, 6, 15, 38, 70, 73, 75, 85,
97, 112, 137, 138, 147, 148, 149, 150, 151
Exodus, book of 8, 12, 16, 25, 35, 63–8
exodus, the 16, 21, 22, 28, 62–9, 76
Ezekiel, prophet 21, 138, 147, 150
Ezekiel the Tragedian 1, 62–9, 87
Ezra 2, 8, 21, 138–9

178